God's Master Performance

The Book of Revelation — Mysteries Unveiled

A Verse-By-Verse Study of God's Grand Finale

EDGAR
CAINA
3/8/96

God's Master Performance

The Book of Revelation — Mysteries Unveiled

A Verse-By-Verse Study of God's Grand Finale

by

Hilton Sutton

HARRISON HOUSE
Tulsa, Oklahoma

2nd Printing

GOD'S MASTER PERFORMANCE — *The Book of Revelation* — *Mysteries Unveiled* — *A Verse-By-Verse Study of God's Grand Finale*
ISBN 0-89274-740-4
Revised Edition of previous title, *REVELATION* — *God's Grand Finale*, ISBN 0-89274-298-4
Copyright © 1984, 1995 by Hilton Sutton
Mission to America
736 Wilson Road
Humble, Texas 77338

Published by Harrison House, Inc.
P. O. Box 35035
Tulsa, Oklahoma 74153

Dedication

For the believing Church.

My thanks to God the Father, the Holy Spirit and our Lord Jesus for Their supernatural help. Also, I thank my family for their patience during the years of preparation and my staff for the help they afforded me.

To God be the glory!

Contents

Preface

Present world affairs are causing the ancient prophecies of the Holy Scriptures to rapidly come to pass. Prophecies pertaining to the restoration of Israel set the stage for the return of Samaria, Judea and Jerusalem to Israel. This fulfillment occurred during the Six-Day War of 1967.

These same prophetic fulfillments have brought us closer to prophetic events found within the book of Revelation. I hasten to point out that the prophecies within the book of Revelation are not yet being fulfilled.

Daniel writes about the "time of the end" in chapter 12. This term *time of the end* identifies the closing of the vast period known as "the last days." From the prophecies of Joel 2:28-31, confirmed by Acts 2:16-20, we know the Upper-Room experience was indeed a last-days event. Therefore, we are nearing the completion of 2,000 years of last days. The seven years identified as the Tribulation are also part of the last days. Prophecies, beginning in Revelation 6 with the opening of the first seal by Jesus, get the Tribulation underway.

However, do not overlook and pay only light attention to the first five chapters. They are vitally important to one's understanding of this exciting, dramatic and thrilling book.

Chapter 1 is the chapter of introduction. Pay close attention. Chapters 2 and 3 hold extremely important messages for today's Church. The catching up of the Church (the Rapture) is described by John at the beginning of chapter 4; while the remainder of the chapter, plus chapter 5, reveals personalities, groups and events before the throne of God. These chapters clearly establish the presence of the Church in heaven before the beginning of the Tribulation.

One must conclude that the present fulfillment of prophecies are taking us closer by the day to the catching up of the Church. Remember, the same prophecies which announce the time for the Antichrist and the Tribulation also hasten the day of the glorious appearing of Jesus for the purpose of receiving a glorious Church unto Himself. (1 Thess. 4:16-18; Eph. 5:27.)

The book of Revelation is the greatest book in the Bible, because it contains God's grand conclusion. The utter defeat of Satan's best plan is beautifully described within this glorious book.

Do not allow Satan to keep you from studying this book. It is the one book of the Bible he hates most. He works overtime to keep God's people in ignorance of this important book.

It is time *you* understand and are blessed by the content of the book of Revelation.

Introduction

The most dramatic, exciting and important book of the Bible is also the most feared, misquoted and declared confusing. Of course, "Revelation" is the title of that book.

No one questions the drama and excitement of this magnificent volume, but they may question that it is the most important book in the Bible. Why so?

As you know from experience, no author places his grand finale or climax at any place in his book except the last chapter. Were an author to do otherwise, few would finish reading his book. Anything written after the grand finale or climax would be anticlimactic, downhill and of little interest.

God, being perfect and the greatest Author of all, got it right the first time. He places the grand finale of His Word in the last book of the Bible: The Revelation.

Since this is an absolute, it elevates the book of Revelation to a very important position. You will discover that it brings together many great truths of the Bible. It fills in the missing pieces and harmonizes various biblical teachings. It is indeed the *Grand Finale of God's Word*.

How delighted and happy I became when I discovered Jesus was the One in control of all the events revealed in this book, and that reading the book of Revelation brings blessings, according to chapter 1, verse 3. As you study, you will understand this statement; and it is absolutely important that you do.

I am grateful to the Holy Spirit for His help in enabling me to properly and positively present this glorious

Revelation. God the Father gets all the glory, and I remain just one of His many servants. I am extremely blessed that He has chosen me for this assignment.

Approach this book with an open heart, inviting the Holy Spirit to illuminate your understanding and let the blessings flow.

PART I
Keys to Understanding Revelation

1

Why Study Revelation?

You never put down a book without reading the last chapter or leave a play as the closing act is about to begin.

The Revelation is the final book of the sixty-six volumes which compose the Bible. It is the last chapter of the most exciting, provocative book you could ever read, the closing act of the play of plays, the grand finale of a master performance. As a whole, the Church has "walked out" on it.

Through one of His angels, the Lord Jesus Christ Himself gave The Revelation to the apostle John.

The Time Is At Hand

The Revelation was important to the Church in early Bible days, and it is just as important to us today. Revelation 1:3 ends with, **for the time is near [at hand KJV]**. After John received The Revelation, he sent it to the churches in Asia so that it might be distributed among the saints and passed down to us.

It is imperative for every believer to understand The Revelation. It was not designed to confuse the saints. However, they need to give their attention to its explanation. Today as God opens His servants' minds to the full understanding of the vision first given to John, there is a growing interest in it. God is using several persons to teach this message. No one man can claim credit for what the Holy Spirit is doing.

You may have heard renowned theologians and teachers disagree over Revelation's true interpretation.

Some of them say it is not significant today because its prophecies have already been fulfilled. Others say it is not to be understood until some later date. Still others say it reveals a terrible future and should be left alone.

Often, people comment simply that they cannot begin to grasp its meaning. They say, "If most great scholars and godly men don't understand Revelation, certainly I never will," or "I don't need to understand Revelation. After Jesus catches up the Church, I won't be here when the things it describes happen."

This attitude is a cop-out, to use popular terminology. Revelation 1:3 instructs us to **keep those things which are written in it**. One must understand Revelation in order to be able to keep the things written within it.

God would not give us a delightfully uncomplicated book, then close it with a chapter draped in such theological profoundness that no two people could agree on its meaning.

In defense of this majestic book, please consider these next statements.

God would never design anything with intent to confuse or disturb you. Revelation is not a confusing book. Remember, God is *not* the author of confusion. (1 Cor. 14:33.) It is Satan who creates confusion, not God. For anyone to declare Revelation confusing would be tantamount to making Satan its author.

As Scripture states, the Word is spiritually discerned and is foolishness to the carnal or natural man. (1 Cor. 2:14.) Do not allow to enter your mind the kind of thoughts which say, "This isn't as important a book as are the other sixty-five."

Paul wrote to Timothy: **All Scripture** (including Revelation) **is given by inspiration of God, and is profitable for doctrine, for reproof, for correction, for**

instruction in righteousness, that the man (or woman) **of God may be complete, thoroughly equipped for every good work** (2 Tim. 3:16,17).

We have no choice but to recognize the value of Revelation for *doctrine,* for *reproof,* for *correction,* and for its great influence on *righteous instructions.*

The Word of God is set forth to teach, correct and instruct. The Revelation is profitable. God gave it to us to prepare us for the Christian walk. You and I can never become thoroughly furnished, or equipped, to do God's work without a good understanding of the book of Revelation.

Through the ages, many have worked for God while being only partially equipped. Thank God for what they have accomplished; but had they been thoroughly equipped, they would have been even more successful.

To become so completely made ready to do all good works does require study of God's Word. Such study begins in Genesis and is completed in the last chapter of Revelation.

United States Army recruiters use the theme, "Be all that you can be — in the Army." According to Second Timothy 2:3,4, we too are an army. We should strive to be the best (1 Cor. 9:24-27); and to do so, we must embrace all of God's Word. Every believer has a favorite verse, chapter or book; but one cannot develop a fully equipped and mature Christian life on just that small part of Scripture.

There can be no question about Satan's hatred for the book of Revelation. He has opposed it in every conceivable manner. For many believers, he has successfully kept them away from or out of this book by one means or another.

One person will cop out on reading material about which he or she is either misinformed or totally ignorant.

Another will say, "Well, I read the last chapter and we win...so?"

Another favorite cop-out is, "It really doesn't matter what I believe. God's got everything planned, and it will come out just that way."

Cop-outs of this type only reveal a lack of knowledge of the very Book these people confess to believe.

Through the years, I have discovered one of Satan's best methods for keeping the majority of the Church community confused about or totally out of the book of Revelation: by making it a book of *doom and gloom*. Please take note of a very important instruction the Holy Spirit provides through the apostle Paul:

> **How is it then, brethren? Whenever you come together** (a meeting of believers), **each of you has a psalm, has a teaching, has a tongue, has a revelation, has an interpretation. Let all things be done for edification.**
>
> **1 Corinthians 14:26**

The word *edify* means to build up or equip. Every church service should edify the believer. He or she should leave better equipped to serve God and win others. If something is done or taught in a service that does not edify, the believers will have been shortchanged or weakened rather than strengthened.

All things must edify, and that includes the presentation of the majestic book of Revelation. It cannot be a book of doom and gloom, as such does not edify.

I grew up hearing The Revelation as a doom-and-gloom message. I may have learned a few things about that book, but my spirit man was left unedified.

After entering the ministry in 1950, I began a serious study of the book of Revelation. I thank God for those under whose ministry I sat through the years. Although with their method of presentation they painted a horrible picture of the future, I still learned from them.

True, I was not edified; I was often frightened out of my wits, yet I learned.

Sometimes the teacher made the Antichrist larger than Jesus, and Satan almost equal to God. Other things were also taught which were not biblically sound, such as how the Antichrist will rule the world and all who are left on the earth will take the mark of the Beast. As you study, you will discover as I did that neither of the above points is true.

God does not cause fear. **For God has not given us a spirit of fear, but of power and of love and of a sound mind** (2 Tim. 1:7). He would not conclude His Word with a frightening story.

Adopt a positive approach in your study of Revelation. You can understand it; it is not complicated. Make this confession:

The Revelation is God's Word. God has set it forth for me. By faith, I am going to reach into God's Word and assimilate it into my inner man.

Determine to accomplish this under the direction of the Holy Spirit.

Examine Scriptures in Context

When studying God's Word, follow this rule: *Take no Scriptures out of their original setting.* When we examine a few Scriptures in relation to the whole Bible, we can easily discern their true meaning. Consequently, we are **rightly dividing the word of truth** (2 Tim. 2:15).

After examining Scriptures out of context, people tend to draw final conclusions that are different from the ones God intended. This explains why Revelation mystifies so many people.

Before I began studying Revelation, I had heard mostly negative teachings about it. However, God impressed upon me that if I would pursue the study of this book, He would open the true meaning to me.

To begin, I purchased several volumes on Revelation. As I examined them, my interest faded. God did not wish my thinking to be clouded. These books, which failed to inform the readers as to what God commanded concerning this prophecy, certainly did not excite them about living today in the end times. God wanted me to study the Word itself.

Those who refer to The Revelation as "a book of hidden meanings" violate the title that God Himself chose. The word *revelation* means "that which is revealed or made clearly visible."

The further I proceeded into Revelation, the more clearly I understood it. After my first few readings, I began to receive pieces of understanding from the Holy Spirit. Finally, the jigsaw puzzle of understood details fit into a single unit: After years of study, I clearly understood The Revelation from the first to the last verse.

A Book of Blessings

God promises a blessing to those who read Revelation:

> **The Revelation of Jesus Christ, which God gave Him to show His servants — things which must shortly take place. And He sent and signified it by His angel to His servant John, who bore witness to the word of God, and to the testimony of Jesus Christ, to all things that he saw.**
>
> ***Blessed is he who reads and those who hear** the words of this prophecy, and keep those things which are written in it; for the time is near.*
>
> **Revelation 1:1-3**

Personally, I have discovered the truth of the statement: **Blessed is he who reads and those who hear the words of**

this prophecy. The audiences to whom I have taught Revelation have also been greatly blessed.

Follow this advice when teaching Revelation:

Conduct the sessions on consecutive evenings, urging your congregation to be present at every one.

Major on the role of Jesus and God's master performance rather than on the Antichrist and mark of the Beast.

Teach in a simple, positive, enthusiastic manner, staying away from speculation and sensationalism. The content of the book itself is sensational. Prophecy teachers have long been known for their speculation, which often draws attention to what they don't know. This statement is not intended to be judgmental, but a positive critique of methods normally used.

With much help from the Holy Spirit in more than thirty years of study, I have carefully avoided the theological snares of past methods of interpretation. What you are about to read is simple, positive, dramatic, stimulating and true. I can promise you that you will be edified, not frightened.

Study Revelation — understand it and claim your blessing. You will discover that it is a book full of blessings.

From John's information concerning himself, we learn a vitally important lesson. He revealed that he had been exiled from the mainland to the isle of Patmos in the Aegean Sea. That was not a great place then, and it is not too sought after today. John was in his mid-nineties when exiled. We must pay attention to his statement in verse 10 of chapter 1:

I was in the Spirit on the Lord's Day.

John maintained his spiritual life, regardless of circumstances or adverse conditions. Because he refused to

allow adversity to interfere with his relationship to the
Father, Son and Holy Spirit, he remained blessed of God.

2
Five Keys

Within Revelation are five keys which unlock its meaning. It also contains the master key necessary to unlock other "obscure" passages of the Bible. This proves that we are to give The Revelation as much attention as we do the rest of God's Word.

Key One: The Revelation of Jesus

The Revelation of Jesus Christ, **which God gave Him to show His servants — things which must shortly take place....**

Revelation 1:1

Most godly men teach only part of Revelation. They discuss the period of plagues and tragedies, the Antichrist system of government, the mark of the Beast and the Battle of Armageddon. But it is *Jesus,* not these catastrophies, Who dominates this book.

Some translations use the title, "The Revelation of St. John the Divine." This is a misnomer. The Revelation is the "revealing" or "unveiling" of Jesus Christ. John was the first of many who were to understand.

Since Jesus is the central theme of Revelation, one can understand the blessing attached to this great prophecy.

Three Views of Jesus

The New Testament records three views of Jesus.

From the Gospels — Matthew, Mark, Luke and John — we visualize Jesus Christ the Man: He Who came to save

21

the lost. Millions of church people know Jesus only as Savior.

From the Epistles, particularly those written by the apostle Paul, we visualize Jesus as the Head of the Church. We see Him as He relates daily with His followers. Many believers know the Christ of the Gospels and the Epistles.

The Revelation gives us the third dimension to complete our view of the Lord. From this book, we visualize Jesus as the triumphant Lord. We learn that, as King of kings and Lord of lords, Jesus will rule over His unending kingdom on earth. Knowing Jesus in His fullness is very exciting.

Key Two: The Believer's Right to Understand Revelation

Once again, let's look at Revelation 1:1:

> **The Revelation of Jesus Christ,** *which God gave Him to show His servants* **— things which must shortly take place....**

Servants is plural. Some translations omit the second "s." This is unfortunate and misleading. *Servant*, singular, implies that John was blessed above all men. But John was the first of many to whom the understanding of The Revelation was to come. The second key is this: Jesus has given us, His servants, the biblical right to understand and enjoy the book of Revelation.

The apostle Paul instructs us to study the Word: **Study to shew thyself approved unto God, a workman that needeth not to be ashamed, rightly dividing the word of truth** (2 Tim. 2:15 KJV).

The New Testament tells us that the Holy Spirit will teach us the truth and open our understanding of the Word: **However, when He, the Spirit of truth, has come, He will guide you into all truth; for He will not speak on His own** *authority,* **but whatever He hears He will speak; and He will tell you things to come** (John 16:13).

When the Holy Spirit directed my vision to it, I discovered the second "s" in *servants*. I suddenly realized that, in the same way the Holy Spirit showed me that magnificant "s," He would give me a complete understanding of the book of Revelation! Because of the plurality of *servants, you* have a biblical right to understand the book of Revelation.

Key Three: Parallel Accounts of Heaven and Earth

Revelation's chapter divisions separate two stories which parallel one another. One occurs in heaven, the other on earth; both take place during a seven-year period.

The following passage fixes this seven-year time frame:

> **Seventy weeks are determined for your people and for your holy city, to finish the transgression, to make an end of sins, to make reconciliation for iniquity, to bring in everlasting righteousness, to seal up vision and prophecy, and to anoint the Most Holy.**
>
> **Know therefore and understand, that from the going forth of the command to restore and build Jerusalem until Messiah the Prince, there shall be seven weeks and sixty-two weeks; the street shall be built again, and the wall, even in troublesome times.**
>
> **And after the sixty-two weeks Messiah shall be cut off, but not for Himself; and the people of the prince who is to come shall destroy the city and the sanctuary. The end of it shall be with a flood, and till the end of the war desolations are determined.**
>
> **Daniel 9:24-26**

Daniel speaks of the seventy weeks of God's determined dealings with the nation of Israel. Each day of those weeks is one year long. Careful examination of this passage reveals that the events it describes cover years and could not possibly occur in the same number of days. The seventy weeks cover a period of 490 years rather than 490 days.

Daniel tells us when the period begins and at what point there is a break. The break comes at the close of the sixty-ninth week when Jesus the Prince enters Jerusalem and is rejected by those He comes to save. This leaves only one week, the seventieth, for future fulfillment. Since each day equals one year, this last week actually covers a seven-year period.

The Church Age occurs between the sixty-ninth and seventieth weeks. It began with the ministry of Christ and ends with the Rapture of the Church. Since the Church Age is the same as the kingdom of God on earth (Luke 16:16), we know its beginning. We also know it ends with the Rapture which precedes God's last seven years of work with Israel. (See Rom. 11:25.) Presently, we are living in this **time of the end** (Dan. 12:4). (Daniel's term **time of the end** should not carry a connotation of doom. It simply indicates that the Church Age is closing.)

At the end of the Church Age — the seventieth and final week of Daniel's prophecy — "the Tribulation Period" begins. The book of Daniel informs us about this period. The book of Revelation confirms the truth in Daniel, then describes the details of the activities occurring in heaven and on earth during this time.

The story of heaven is described in Revelation 4, 5, 19 and 20; the story of earth in Revelation 6, 8, 9, 16, 19 and 20. Chapters 4 and 5 reveal the activities of the people and angels around God's throne. We make an easy transition from the heavenly story in chapter 5 to the earthly story in chapter 6. The description of earth's activities during the years of the Tribulation originates in this chapter.

A lapse of continuity follows chapter 6. Chapters 8 and 9 continue the earthly story from chapter 6. Chapter 16 again picks up the earthly story. Chapter 19 begins with the heavenly story, then makes a quick transition to the earthly one. Chapter 20 continues with the earthly story, then concludes with the heavenly one.

Key Four: Informational Chapters

The remaining chapters do not necessarily aid the continuity of the two unfolding stories, but add information. Instead of continuing the immediate story, occasionally one of these chapters enlarges upon details concerning a person, group of people or particular event occurring in one of the stories.

When writing about a particular geographical area, one would first write a wide variety of cameo stories about the area's outstanding individuals, families and events. When incorporating the cameo stories into one major story, however, the writer would weave them together with the central theme of the chosen area. This is the way the book of Revelation is written.

The informational chapters are 7, 10-15, 17 and 18. Chapters 20, 21 and 22 describe the events occurring after the seven-year period: the thousand-year reign of Christ, the new heavens, the new earth and the New Jerusalem. Although they share information of the glorious future, they do not fit in the category of informational chapters.

Throughout this book, each chapter is labeled as to whether it concerns the earthly or heavenly story or is informational.

Key Five:
Past, Present and Future Events

Write the things which you have seen, and the things which are, and the things which will take place after this.

Revelation 1:19

We can see from these instructions to John that the book of Revelation describes past, present and future events.

Historians vs. Futurists

In the theological world there are two major schools of thought concerning the interpretation of Revelation: historian and futurist.

The historian declares and attempts to show that events in history have already fulfilled the prophecy of Revelation. He concludes that Revelation is of no significance to us today.

If the events in Revelation have already come to pass, we are living in the glorious 1,000-year reign of righteousness and peace on earth. But "a reign of peace" does not describe conditions on earth today. The historical events of Revelation tie the future to the past and further establish the Bible as a complete record of God's plan.

The futurist teaches that events in chapters 4 through 22 are unfulfilled. The story created on this presumption does not correlate with events of the Old and New Testaments. It contains missing pieces and lacks harmony. Both the historian and the futurist have overlooked the reference to past, present and future in Revelation 1:19.

No Contradictions

The Bible is composed of sixty-six volumes written by some forty men of God over a period of more than 1,600 years. The Bible's continuity is superb. Despite what liberal theologians have said (usually to cover their own lack of understanding), there are no contradictions in the Bible.

God manifests and moves in patterns. This is one way in which He is able to convince us of His presence. He declares in Malachi 3:6, **For I am the Lord, I do not change.** God, Who is steadfast, does not break His patterns.

Since the previous sixty-five books of the Bible fit together and support one another, Revelation must fit the same pattern. To tell the future, Revelation must have the support of the past — there must be a definite link in the overall story. If there were no link, liberal theologians could declare that Revelation is not a part of the canon of Scripture, but was added at some later time.

We will see that Revelation contains numerous references to past events drawn out of the Old and New Testaments. These support the story being told and lay a solid foundation for future events.

Summary

Key One: The central theme of Revelation is the revealing of Jesus Christ.

Key Two: Jesus' servants are to understand this revelation.

Key Three: The stories of the events in heaven and on earth during the Tribulation Period are woven around the central theme of Jesus.

Key Four: The informational chapters provide more details about the stories of heaven and earth.

Key Five: The events in Revelation occur in the past, present and future.

PART II
Letters to the Seven Churches

3

Revelation 1
The Cover Letter

Chapter 1 introduces Revelation. We learn how and where John received the prophecy. This chapter also contains a large portion of the cover letter which John wrote to the seven churches in Asia.

John sent each church three items:

- A copy of the prophecy.

- A cover letter explaining how he received the prophecy and his reason for sending it.

- A letter dictated to him by the Lord Jesus Christ which contained instructions for each church. (These letters are recorded in Rev. 2 and 3.)

The cover letter to the seven churches in Asia begins with John's salutation.

> John, to the seven churches which are in Asia:
> Grace to you and peace from Him who is and who was and who is to come, and from the seven Spirits who are before His throne, and from Jesus Christ, the faithful witness, the firstborn from the dead, and the ruler over the kings of the earth.
> To Him who loved us and washed us from our sins in His own blood, and has made us kings and priests to His God and Father, to Him be glory and dominion forever and ever. Amen.
> Behold, He is coming with clouds, and every eye will see Him, even they who pierced Him. And all the

tribes of the earth will mourn because of Him. Even so, Amen.

"I am the Alpha and the Omega, the Beginning and the End," says the Lord, "who is and who was and who is to come, the Almighty."

Revelation 1:4-8

Since John knew that this letter would travel throughout the churches, he used it to remind them of the many great truths of God's Word. His salutation is filled with Gospel!

John greets the churches for himself and sends greetings from the Holy Spirit (symbolized in v. 4 by **the seven Spirits who are before His** [God's] **throne**). John sends them greetings from Jesus Christ, then describes Jesus in a statement containing no defeat. He closes it by giving glory and praise to the Lord.

The Second Coming

Verse 7 portrays the return of Jesus:

Behold, He is coming with clouds, and every eye will see Him, even they who pierced Him. And all the tribes of the earth will mourn because of Him. Even so, Amen.

The Second Coming of the Lord Jesus Christ is divided into events: His appearing and His return.

The first occurs when Jesus departs the throne of God and appears in the heavens above the earth to wait for the Holy Spirit to resurrect the dead in Christ. Then the living and resurrected saints are caught up together in the clouds and rise to meet the Lord in the air. We call this "the catching up of the Church" or "the Rapture." (The term *rapture*, which does not appear in the Scriptures, means "to be caught up.")

Verse 7 describes Jesus' return to earth, when He takes control of all governments in order to fulfill the prophecies of Isaiah 9:6. He sets up His 1,000-year reign, a time of peace and righteousness, and rules with **a rod of iron** (Rev. 2:27), firm authority. He doesn't rule the Church with firm authority, because its members are like Him. But there are people over whom He must rule in this manner.

Only the true Church will be aware of Jesus' *appearing*. The rest of the world will not know about it until after the saints are gone. When Jesus *returns* to take over all government, **every eye will see Him. And all the tribes of the earth will mourn because of Him** (v. 7).

John ends the salutation by again speaking of Jesus: **"I am the Alpha and the Omega, the Beginning and the End," says the Lord, "who is and who was and who is to come, the Almighty"** (v. 8).

The Exile

Verse 9 continues John's letter:

> **I, John, both your brother and companion in the tribulation and kingdom and patience of Jesus Christ, was on the island that is called Patmos for the word of God and for the testimony of Jesus Christ.**

John explains that he was exiled from the mainland and the company of the saints to the isle of Patmos in the Aegean Sea. The Aegean Sea lies between Greece on the west and Turkey on the east. All seven churches addressed in chapters 2 and 3 were located in the area we today identify as Turkey. John had lost favor with governmental powers and the religious leaders of the day because he preached God's Word and testified of Jesus.

The religious leaders wanted to kill John. History records numerous attempts made on his life, but God gave John divine protection.

Notice that John did not allow natural circumstances and conditions to affect his spiritual welfare or outlook. He says, **I was in the Spirit on the Lord's Day** (v. 10).

Many Christians allow adversity to badly affect their spirituality. Their attitude, confession and testimony become negative. We should never allow adverse circumstances to affect our spiritual relationship with our heavenly Father, Jesus, the Holy Spirit or the company of believers. As followers of Jesus, we can govern circumstances rather than permit them to control us.

John realized that by maintaining his spiritual relationship and proper attitude he would remain elevated above existing circumstances. He was not trying to exercise mind over matter to deny the reality of his exile. He acknowledged it as fact but continued walking in the Spirit, enjoying the attention provided him by Jesus through the Holy Spirit and the angels.

The Lord's Day

John said, **I was in the Spirit on the Lord's Day, and I heard behind me a loud voice, as of a trumpet** (v. 10).

Throughout the New Testament, the Lord's Day is considered the first day of the week, the day on which Jesus arose victorious over death and hell. He had defeated Satan, solved the sin problem and provided complete salvation for the spirits, souls and bodies of all mankind.

We should not regard one day higher than another, because we worship our Lord seven days a week. Under the Old Covenant the last day of the week — the seventh, Saturday — was the Sabbath. Israel worshiped God at the end of the week. Scripture states that Jewish people keep the Sabbath as their way of remembering their covenant with God, originating with Abraham. (See Ex. 31:16,17; Gen. 15:18; 17:2-11.)

As taught by the apostle Paul, the Lord's Day is a part of the New (and better) Covenant. Under the New Covenant, believers began worshiping God on the first day. The Sabbath, or seventh, day should still be a day of rest, but there is no point in making an issue out of minor differences of opinion concerning the Scriptures.

Emphasis on Jesus

John's cover letter continues:

> I was in the Spirit on the Lord's Day, and I heard behind me a loud voice, as of a trumpet, saying, "I am the Alpha and the Omega, the First and the Last," and, "What you see, write in a book and send it to the seven churches which are in Asia: to Ephesus, to Smyrna, to Pergamos, to Thyatira, to Sardis, to Philadelphia, and to Laodicea."
>
> Then I turned to see the voice that spoke with me. And having turned I saw seven golden lampstands, and in the midst of the seven lampstands One like the Son of Man, clothed with a garment down to the feet and girded about the chest with a golden band.
>
> His head and hair were white like wool, as white as snow, and His eyes like a flame of fire; His feet were like fine brass, as if refined in a furnace, and His voice as the sound of many waters;
>
> He had in His right hand seven stars, out of His mouth went a sharp two-edged sword, and His countenance was like the sun shining in its strength.
>
> And when I saw Him, I fell at His feet as dead. But He laid His right hand on me, saying to me, "Do not be afraid; I am the First and the Last. I am He who lives, and was dead, and behold, I am alive forevermore. Amen. And I have the keys of Hades and of Death.
>
> "Write the things which you have seen, and the things which are, and the things which will take place after this.
>
> "The mystery of the seven stars which you saw in My right hand, and the seven golden lampstands: The seven stars are the angels of the seven churches, and the seven lampstands which you saw are the seven churches" (vv. 10-20).

Notice that the Voice which John heard sounded like a trumpet. (v. 10.) When John begins receiving the prophecy, he again describes the Voice that sounds like a trumpet. (Rev. 4:1.) John's emphasis in the cover letter is always on Jesus.

John describes Jesus in detail and states that **out of His mouth went a sharp two-edged sword**. This **two-edged sword** is God's Word.

Jesus' statement that He has **the keys of Hades and of Death** clearly establishes His victorious conquest of hell and death. From the cross Jesus descended into hell where He paid the price for all our sins. Then He crossed into paradise and ministered to the righteous dead to prepare them for their transferal to heaven. As He left Hades (or Sheol), Jesus completely defeated Satan and all his angels, principalities and powers. What an indescribable triumph!

Jesus explains to John the seven stars and the seven lampstands (called **candlesticks** in KJV). The stars are the angels of the seven churches; the lampstands are the seven churches. An angel assigned to each of the seven churches provides angelic assistance to that church in its community. The angel will serve as both messenger and assistant to the pastor. This is a part of God's plan of communication.

The book of Revelation is a great source for the study of angels and their ministry. For additional insight into the ministry of angels, examine Psalm 91:11,12 and Hebrews 1:13,14. The words for *angel* and *pastor* are not interchangeable. Their only common characteristic is that both are messengers.

The lampstand symbolizes representation before the throne of God; the angel is evidence of the angelic assignment in behalf of that church. The angel has the responsibility of seeing that John's letter is delivered to the pastor of each church and to the saints within each region.

People who doubt the existence of angels will be convinced of their existence following a study of Revelation. This book describes how many there are, what they do and for whom they minister. We too have representation before the throne of God. Today, a mighty angel is over every region of the Church, assigned by God to work on behalf of that region.

One Body

The believers of all regions must relate to one another in perfect harmony. The apostle Paul says, **Now indeed there are many members, yet one body** (1 Cor. 12:20). Jesus prayed, **Father, keep through Your name those whom You have given Me,** *that they may be one as We are* (John 17:11). He also prayed:

> **I do not pray for these alone, but also for those who will believe in Me through their word; that they all may be one, as You, Father, are in Me, and I in You; that they also may be one in Us, that the world may believe that You sent Me** (vv. 20,21).

The words you speak about Jesus Christ to others are vitally important. Jesus has already prayed not only for you but also for those you are going to win.

The apostle Paul wrote to the Church, **Now I plead with you, brethren, by the name of our Lord Jesus Christ, that you all speak the same thing, and that there be no divisions among you** (1 Cor. 1:10). The many divisions among God's children have hindered both the preaching of the Gospel and the salvation of many.

The world states: "All you Christians believe that you have the same heavenly Father and Savior. You believe the same Bible and that you are going to the same place when you die. Why are you so divided? Why do you often oppose and fight one another?"

Not only Revelation but the whole Word of God teaches Christian unity. Divisions must not occur within the Christian community.

Paul said to the people of Corinth: **Now I say this, that each of you says, "I am of Paul," or "I am of Apollos," or "I am of Cephas," or "I am of Christ." Is Christ divided? Was Paul crucified for you? Or were you baptized in the name of Paul?** (1 Cor. 1:12,13). He went on to tell them that they were carnal and spiritually immature to allow those divisions to remain among them.

Because of our divisions, we have almost wrecked the Gospel of Jesus Christ for multitudes of people. We have been carnal about our denominational structures, narrow in our beliefs. Some people have gone so far as to imply that unless one is a member of their group, he could not possibly go to heaven!

With the Holy Spirit educating us, we are beginning to mature, but we still have room for improvement! Even though leaders do not teach sectarianism, immature Christians quickly divide, following after one particular preacher or labeling themselves after one particular movement. In addition to denominational divisions, among other divisions, are the evangelical, fundamentalist groups and the Charismatics. They seldom worship together.

Realize that you can disagree without being disagreeable. When the children of God become disagreeable, they are manifesting the wrong spirit. As long as you disagree but continue walking together in love for the common cause, you form a vehicle that the Holy Spirit will use for sweeping multitudes of people into the kingdom of God.

Having a right attitude toward a fellow Christian provides the Holy Spirit opportunity to work in his behalf.

The Holy Spirit will enlighten and correct whoever is "in the wrong." Sometimes when both people involved are a little off-center, He works on each one. Christians should complement, aid and support one another. By flowing together, they are allowing God to provide a spiritual umbrella of protection from those who perpetrate false teachings.

You have the strength and ability to correct someone in error without putting him in condemnation or casting him out. If he doesn't change, follow the instructions in the Scriptures. Set him aside for a season, then go restore him. (See 1 Tim. 3:14,15; Gal. 6:1; Rom. 16:17.) That is the real love of God.

Of the seven churches in Asia, Satan gained a foothold in six of them. To get into our churches today, he uses the same tools that he used then. If members of the Church lose their first love (of Jesus), permit false teachers and doctrines, and speak negative confessions, the devil can either destroy or divide them. Divisions weaken their influence and ability.

We must grow in the grace and knowledge of the Lord. Paul assures us that we will **all come to the unity of the faith and the knowledge of the Son of God, to a perfect man** (Eph. 4:13) and that we will **grow up in all things into Him who is the head — Christ — from whom the whole body, joined and knit together by what every joint supplies...** (vv. 15,16).

Revelation summarizes every point of doctrine in the Bible. It clears up any confusion by completing the teachings of the Old and New Testaments. In addition to studying the prophecy disclosed through Revelation, we will also examine many other beautiful truths.

John clearly establishes that the seven lampstands symbolize the seven churches, each of which should be a "lighthouse"; and the seven stars, angels or messengers.

This explanation ends the introductory chapter of Revelation, setting the stage for the exciting material which follows. We will examine the conclusion of John's letter in our discussion of Revelation 22.

4
Revelation 2
Ephesus, Smyrna, Pergamos, Thyatira

Chapters 2 and 3 record the seven letters to the churches in Asia. In writing these letters John simply served as secretary to the Lord Jesus. Jesus dictated the letters; John wrote them down and sent them to the proper church.

A Pattern of Ministry

The letters reveal a pattern in Jesus' way of dealing with the churches.

First, Jesus commends each church for its characteristics which please Him. He points out faith, patience, works, love, service, hatred for evil and a desire to know the reputation of incoming men.

Second, He calls attention to the things which displease Him, such as loss of first love, wrong confession, false doctrines, false teachers, spiritual death, fear and loss of spiritual power.

Third, without putting any church under condemnation, Jesus calls for repentance. A call to repentance is a work of love, because it looks beyond faults to what can be.

Fourth, Jesus warns of the price to be paid for persistent disobedience. His love again prevails in His warning.

A parent who continually criticizes a child without lovingly telling him how to correct his problems demonstrates no love. The child will be laboring under constant condemnation. The wise parent brags about his child, but also tells him how to improve. Pointing out the disadvantages of disobedience can be a loving act.

The Church of Ephesus

To the angel of the church of Ephesus write, "These things says He who holds the seven stars in His right hand, who walks in the midst of the seven golden lampstands:

"I know your works, your labor, your patience, and that you cannot bear those who are evil. And you have tested those who say they are apostles and are not, and have found them liars; and you have persevered and have patience, and have labored for My name's sake and have not become weary" (vv. 1-3).

This is a church with a positive reputation! However, verse 4 states, **Nevertheless I have this against you, that you have left your first love.** What a charge!

Our first love is for Jesus Christ our Lord. It consists of strong dedication, consecration and commitment. When you first came to know Jesus, were you so excited about Him that you shared Him everywhere? Perhaps some people branded you a fanatic; others said, "One of these days the new will wear off and you'll settle down." If that happened, that is tragic! First love can slip away and be replaced by things.

We become so involved in trying to serve the Lord that we create all kinds of vehicles through which to serve Him. Before we realize it, service organizations, committees and programs can place such a demand on our time that they become first place in our lives.

Luke 10 tells the story of Mary and her sister, Martha. Jesus said to Martha, **You are worried and troubled about**

many things. But one thing is needed, and Mary has chosen that good part, which will not be taken away from her (vv. 41,42). Mary had chosen to sit at Jesus' feet and listen to His words.

Even though the Ephesians centered their activities around Jesus, they relegated Him to second place. Jesus told them: **Remember therefore from where you have fallen; repent and do the first works, or else I will come to you quickly and remove your lampstand from its place —** **unless you repent** (Rev. 2:5).

Jesus clearly pointed out that the most severe consequence of disobedience was the removal of their lampstand, the representation at God's throne, from its place.

Jesus continues His analysis of the Ephesian church: **But this you have, that you hate the deeds of the Nicolaitans, which I also hate** (v. 6). The Nicolaitans had false teachers and error among them. Jesus didn't hate the people; He hated their deeds. They were trying to make an inroad into the churches. They wanted the priesthood to be restored and the church to be controlled by laymen.

Despite their good points, the Ephesians are called to repentance because they have lost their first love. When believers lose their first love, the joy of salvation will also wane. With a loss of joy, one's spiritual strength will diminish. The Scriptures teach that the **joy of the Lord** is our strength (Neh. 8:10), and the psalmist David prayed: **Restore to me the *joy* of Your salvation, and uphold me by Your generous Spirit. Then I will teach transgressors Your ways, and sinners shall be converted to You** (Ps. 51:12,13).

It is simple Bible truth when believers lose their first love; they not only become spiritually weak, but they cease from soulwinning. *Joy of salvation* and *joy in the Holy Ghost* are vital to our everyday walk with Jesus. *Today the Church needs to do what David did — and do it quickly!* Remember, the Church is made up of folks like you and me.

Jesus admonished the church at Ephesus by saying: **He who has an ear, let him hear what the Spirit says to the churches...** (Rev. 2:7). He also makes this statement to the other six churches, encouraging them to be sensitive to the Holy Spirit. (Rev. 2:11,17,29; 3:6,13,22.)

Listen to the Holy Spirit's Voice

After the Church Age began, the Holy Spirit was the predominant influence on the Church. On the Jewish feast day of Pentecost, the Holy Spirit fulfilled a divine assignment. He manifested for the express purpose of energizing the true Church, the Body of Christ. His oversight and strengthening of the Church will continue until He provides a mature and glorious Church and plays His role in its resurrection and catching up.

Since the Holy Spirit is the overseer of the Church, our sensitivity to Him is vital. We must allow Him to open God's Word to us, showing us how to become spiritually mature and how to please God more. He will show us how to keep our faith strong and unpolluted.

Judge All Things

We must be able to identify the Holy Spirit's voice and His activities. There are many spirits in the world. All of them strive to get our attention in order to bring us under their influence.

The apostle Paul taught, **He who is spiritual judges all things** (1 Cor. 2:15). Those who are truly spiritual will not accept something at face value. They will judge it according to Scripture to determine whether it is the Holy Spirit's work before accepting it or becoming involved. Many Christians say, "I have the witness that this is the Holy

Spirit," as a basis for belief. They get themselves in trouble by playing spiritually unsound games.

Read the textbook, the Bible, to find out how to react. Once Christians become scripturally sound, relying on the Holy Spirit can become automatic. Biblical soundness plus Holy Spirit leadership equals overall soundness and safety.

It is God's business, not ours, to judge a person. But God has provided us with some safe methods by which to judge the things a person does. We can judge a teaching, prophetic utterance or any other supposedly spiritual act.

Satan has kept many of us from obeying First Corinthians 2:15 by saying, "Be careful lest you judge someone." Instead of letting the devil talk us out of obeying the Word, we must try every spirit as the Scriptures teach. (1 John 4:1.) The word *try* means "to prove." It certainly does not imply that one should be suspicious, going about as a detective among the saints.

A sign of spiritual maturity is to take the time to judge all things. With the emphasis placed on hearing what the Holy Spirit has to say, use the following guidelines:

Five Points for Judging Things

1. The Holy Spirit exalts no one but Jesus.

Jesus said, **When He, the Spirit of truth, has come, He will guide you into all truth** (John 16:13). Jesus also said, **I am the way, the truth, and the life** (John 14:6). The Holy Spirit speaks of Jesus for our benefit. We must learn the difference between a prophetic utterance and an exhortation. A prophetic utterance foretells facts which can then be examined for truth. An exhortation urgently presents advice based on the Word.

Many utterances begun with "Thus saith the Lord..." are not prophecies, but exhortations. If these utterances exalt a person or group, they are coming out of the human spirit. In passing judgment, ask if Jesus was exalted.

2. The Holy Spirit always directs attention to Jesus.

To my knowledge there is no biblical record of the Holy Spirit ever drawing attention to Himself, but always to Jesus. The Holy Spirit serves as teacher and amplifier of all that Jesus was, did and taught.

3. The Holy Spirit never violates God's Word.

Every form of prophecy — utterance, dream, vision or revelation — must be substantiated by God's Word. Paul instructs us that prophecy must edify, exhort or comfort. (1 Cor. 14:3.) *The Word of God — not the prophetic utterance, dream, vision or revelation — is the final authority.*

Points 1, 2 and 3 are based on Jesus' teachings recorded in John 14-16.

John 1:1 reads, **In the beginning was the Word, and the Word was with God, and the Word was God.** Verse 14 declares, **And the Word became flesh and dwelt among us.** Jesus is not only the *origin* of the Word, He *is* the Word. The Holy Spirit would not violate nor supersede the Word — Jesus. Because the Holy Spirit brought the written Word into existence, God has no reason to work contrary to it.

Some people say that anything they speak by the name of the Lord and under the authority of the Holy Spirit is as important as the written Word. This is the same as adding to or taking from the Word, which is forbidden. (See Rev. 22:18,19.)

4.The Holy Spirit does everything unto edification.

The apostle Paul wrote, **Let all things be done for edification** (1 Cor. 14:26). The Holy Spirit never overpowers or burdens; never brings fear, depression or despair. He challenges and builds you up; He desires to charge you like a battery and equip you for all good works. When you are under the influence of the Holy Spirit, you continually edify your fellow believers.

5. The work of the Holy Spirit withstands all examination.

The Scriptures teach us to try, prove and examine God, to taste and see that He is good, to try the spirits to see if they are of Him. (1 Cor. 2:15; Mal. 3:10; Ps. 34:8; 1 John 4:1.)

The Holy Spirit is delighted when we obey Scripture; He welcomes our examination of His works. It may take a day, a week or longer to determine whether what was said or done was of the Holy Spirit.

The Holy Spirit gently leads. If a spirit is driving or hurrying you, telling you that unless you accept its statement immediately you will miss God, it is not the Holy Spirit.

If a person through whom a word or action has come is resentful of examination, he is acting by the wrong spirit. Whenever someone offers to prophesy or give you "a word from God," tell that person that, after hearing the word, you will examine it and determine its soundness.

If you do not use these five points to judge all things, you open yourself to possible deception by any of the erroneous spirits at work against the Church. Do not accept anything without judging it.

You Are an Overcomer

Revelation 2:7 continues:

> ...To him who overcomes I will give to eat from the tree of life, which is in the midst of the Paradise of God.

In addition to emphasizing sensitivity to the Spirit, each of the seven letters contains a statement to the overcomer. This indicates that overcomers were in each church, including the one at Sardis that Satan had destroyed. Today overcomers are also in every church.

The seven statements made to the overcomers in the letters to the churches follow:

1. **To him who *overcomes* I will give to eat from the tree of life, which is in the midst of the Paradise of God** (Rev. 2:7).

2. **He who *overcomes* shall not be hurt by the second death** (Rev. 2:11).

3. **To him who *overcomes* I will give some of the hidden manna to eat. And I will give him a white stone, and on the stone a new name written which no one knows except him who receives it** (Rev. 2:17).

4. **And he who *overcomes*, and keeps My works until the end, to him I will give power over the nations — "He shall rule them with a rod of iron; they shall be dashed to pieces like the potter's vessels" — as I also have received from My Father; and I will give him the morning star** (Rev. 2:26-28).

5. **He who *overcomes* shall be clothed in white garments, and I will not blot out his name from the Book of Life; but I will confess his name before My Father and before His angels** (Rev. 3:5).

6. **He who *overcomes*, I will make him a pillar in the temple of My God, and he shall go out no more. I will write on him the name of My God and the name of the city of My God, the New Jerusalem, which comes down out of heaven from My God. And I will write on him My new name** (Rev. 3:12).

7. **To him who *overcomes* I will grant to sit with Me on My throne, as I also overcame and sat down with My Father on His throne** (Rev. 3:21).

Once a person recognizes his need for Jesus, then makes his initial move, he begins overcoming Satan. When his action brings him to the point of accepting Jesus as Savior and Lord, he has overcome! From then on, he overcomes daily as he walks with Jesus. To enable us to successfully overcome, Jesus said, "My Father and I will abide in you." (John 14:23.) The Holy Spirit plus the authority of the Word make this a reality. Jesus said, **If you abide in Me, and My words abide in you, you will ask what you desire, and it shall be done for you** (John 15:7).

Consider these biblical facts: When one accepts Jesus, he overcomes Satan; therefore, he is reborn as an overcomer. By the power of the Holy Spirit, God's Word, personal testimony, the blood of the Lamb, and angelic ministry, one continues overcoming daily. The overcomer always succeeds!

Some have reasoned that they are not overcomers, because Satan still tempts or buffets them as Paul was buffeted. (See 2 Cor. 12:7.) Consequently they forever strive to become what God says they already are.

Accept the truth. You are a new creature. He that is within you is greater than he that is in the world. Since God is for you, the devil is up against Him. You can do all things because of Jesus and His strength.[1]

Jesus said, **I have overcome the world** (John 16:33). Paul said, **We are more than conquerors through Him who loved us** (Rom. 8:37). Choose to believe what God's Word says about you rather than the strange theology which appeals to your carnal mind. Your confession is extremely important, because you are what you confess to be. As you begin confessing what the Word says, you create an atmosphere in which God works to lift you above the circumstances that exist. Confess, "I'm an overcomer!"

---

[1] 2 Corinthians 5:17; 1 John 4:4; Romans 8:31; Philippians 4:13.

The Church of Smyrna

The second letter went to the church of Smyrna.

> And to the angel of the church in Smyrna write, "These things says the First and the Last, who was dead, and came to life:
>
> "I know your works, tribulation, and poverty (but you are rich); and I know the blasphemy of those who say they are Jews and are not, but are a synagogue of Satan.
>
> "Do not fear any of those things which you are about to suffer. Indeed, the devil is about to throw some of you into prison, that you may be tested, and you will have tribulation ten days. Be faithful until death, and I will give you the crown of life.
>
> "He who has an ear, let him hear what the Spirit says to the churches. He who overcomes shall not be hurt by the second death" (vv. 8-11).

Again notice the emphasis upon hearing the Spirit and the statement to the overcomer. People blasphemed saying they were Jews of **a synagogue of Satan**. Some of the people in the church were threatened with imprisonment.

The Lord said, "Even if they imprison you, it will be for a short time. If you lose your life because you have been faithful, I will give you a crown of life." He is encouraging them to be overcomers in the circumstances.

The Church of Pergamos

In the letter to the third church we read:

> And to the angel of the church in Pergamos write, "These things says He who has the sharp two-edged sword:
>
> "'I know your works, and where you dwell, where Satan's throne is. And you hold fast to My name, and did not deny My faith even in the days in which Antipas was My faithful martyr, who was killed among you, where Satan dwells'" (vv. 12,13).

This church seemed like a good church. It had works —
a miracle in itself, considering its location in a very wicked
area. (One of its people, Antipas, had even been martyred.)
In spite of the adversity, the people of the church did not
deny their faith and held fast to the name *Jesus*. This is
extremely commendable. Look, though, at the next verses:

> **But I have a few things against you, because you
> have there those who hold the doctrine of Balaam, who
> taught Balak to put a stumbling block before the
> children of Israel, to eat things sacrificed to idols, and
> to commit sexual immorality. Thus you also have those
> who hold the doctrine of the Nicolaitans, which thing I
> hate** (vv. 14,15).

Again notice that the Lord did not say He hated the
people; He hated their doctrines, their teaching, the error
they were spreading among God's children. Because of this
error, they were in a weakened position in an area where
Satan's manifestation was evident.

Paul says, **But where sin abounded, grace abounded
much more** (Rom. 5:20). When going into a city known to
be wicked, you must maintain a positive godly attitude.
Say, "Praise God, I'm going into an area where the Lord is
really showing Himself! I will be an additional vessel for
God to work through!" You should look forward to these
opportunities of Christian service.

The church of Pergamos had come under the influence
of false teachers. The Lord says to them:

> **Repent, or else I will come to you quickly and will
> fight against them with the sword of My mouth** (the
> Word). **He who has an ear, let him hear what the Spirit
> says to the churches...** (vv. 16,17).

To the overcomer He says:

> **...To him who overcomes I will give some of the
> hidden manna to eat. And I will give him a white stone,
> and on the stone a new name written which no one
> knows except him who receives it** (v. 17).

Again Jesus places emphasis upon listening to the Spirit and reveals the rewards of the overcomer.

The Church of Thyatira

And to the angel of the church in Thyatira write, "These things says the Son of God, who has eyes like a flame of fire, and His feet like fine brass: I know your works, love, service, faith, and your patience; and as for your works, the last are more than the first" (vv. 18,19).

This sounds like a description of a fine church. But this passage continues in verse 20:

"Nevertheless I have a few things against you, because you allow that woman Jezebel, who calls herself a prophetess [God did not call this false teacher a prophetess — she called herself one]**, to teach and seduce My servants to commit sexual immorality and to eat things sacrificed to idols. And I gave her time to repent of her sexual immorality, and she did not repent.**

"Indeed I will cast her into a sickbed, and those who commit adultery with her into great tribulation, unless they repent of their deeds. I will kill her children with death, and all the churches shall know that I am He who searches the minds and hearts. And I will give to each one of you according to your works.

"Now to you I say, and to the rest in Thyatira, as many as do not have this doctrine, who have not known the depths of Satan, as they say, I will put on you no other burden. But hold fast what you have till I come" (vv. 20-25).

This church had a great reputation, but they permitted a woman named Jezebel to teach a false doctrine that seduced God's children into violating His Word. God said that He would deal with Jezebel very harshly. Then He instructed those in Thyatira who had not participated in the sin or condoned her doctrine to hold fast to the good that they had.

Be cautious of those among you whom you do not know. Should you listen to them, remember to judge their teaching carefully. If part of the teaching is erroneous, put all of it away from you. Do not change your views.

Unless truth is being perverted, there can never be error. Teachers like Jezebel appear spiritual and always claim great insight into the things of God. However, deceived themselves, they are able to deceive others because of their abilities as teachers.

Assemble Together

The church of Thyatira was another of the six churches in error. Some people, unable to find the "perfect church," don't go to church. They substitute listening to tapes, reading books and praying. All of these things are good, provided they do not replace fellowship with other believers and study of God's Word.

We should not forsake the **assembling of ourselves together** (Heb. 10:25). This is important and will become more so in our rapid approach toward the day of Jesus' appearing. Every believer must be part of a fellowship of God's children in his community and accept whatever role God assigns there.

Be cautious of any attitude which causes you to assume that you are too spiritual for other Christians. The more spiritual you are, the more you can assist others in their growth. The greater your spirituality, the greater your responsibility for others. God's blessings are heavy upon many churches which are imperfect in the eyes of people.

5

Revelation 3
Sardis, Philadelphia, Laodicea

The Church of Sardis

Despite the inroads Satan made into six of the churches, he was able to destroy only the church at Sardis.

> And to the angel of the church in Sardis write, "These things says He who has the seven Spirits of God and the seven stars: 'I know your works, that you have a name that you are alive, but you are dead.
>
> 'Be watchful, and strengthen the things which remain, that are ready to die, for I have not found your works perfect before God.
>
> 'Remember therefore how you have received and heard; hold fast and repent. Therefore if you will not watch, I will come upon you as a thief, and you will not know what hour I will come upon you.
>
> 'You have a few names even in Sardis who have not defiled their garments; and they shall walk with Me in white, for they are worthy'" (vv. 1-4).

Some saints who remained in this church did their best to serve God under adverse conditions. Jesus declared that He wanted those faithful ones with Him because of their worthiness.

Jesus told the Church as a whole to repent and return to Him. He warned that otherwise it would be too late; He will come back unexpectedly. Verse 3 states: **Therefore if you will not watch, I will come upon you as a thief, and you will not know what hour I will come upon you.**

A similar statement made by Jesus is recorded in Luke 21:36: **Watch therefore, and pray always that you may be counted worthy to escape....**

Jesus said that he who overcomes and continues to overcome shall never have his name blotted out of the Book of Life.

He who overcomes shall be clothed in white garments, and I will not blot out his name from the Book of Life; but I will confess his name before My Father and before His angels (v. 5).

This statement does not support the teaching that, no matter how you live, once your name is in the Lord's Book, it will never be blotted out. Notice that the statement is made to the overcomer, not to one who has been overcome.

The Church of Philadelphia

The church of Philadelphia was the only one of the seven into which Satan had been unable to make an inroad.

And to the angel of the church in Philadelphia write, "These things says He who is holy, He who is true, 'He who has the key of David, He who opens and no one shuts, and shuts and no one opens':

"I know your works. See, I have set before you an open door, and no one can shut it; for you have a little strength, have kept My word, and have not denied My name" (vv. 7,8).

This church confessed that they kept the Word of God. They knew that God's Word is of utmost importance.

Study the Word

Every Christian should have a good working knowledge of the Word obtained through prayerful study. Knowing the Word is vital. It gives you security against believing false teaching and many so-called prophecies, dreams and visions. When these things do not line up with God's Word, you can dismiss them. But if you do not know the Word, you cannot judge such things. You will likely believe them, only to wonder later how you became so misguided.

Instead of lightly reading the Bible, you must study it. Otherwise, you will not comprehend its marvelous truth. To learn the Word of God, meditate it day and night (Josh. 1:8), inviting the aid of the Holy Spirit. You will be blessed in your studies.

Use a number of good translations, a dictionary and an analytical concordance which contains Hebrew and Greek dictionaries. Both children and wayfaring (unlearned) men are able to understand the Scriptures.[1] In other words, the Bible is not hard to understand.

One doesn't need to know Greek, Hebrew, Aramaic and Latin in order to accurately interpret God's Word. When you prayerfully meditate, you will receive from the Lord insight into His Word — including the book of Revelation.

The Philadelphians' Firm Position

The Philadelphians kept God's Word and did not deny the name of Jesus. They also used their strength to carry forth the outreach assigned to them. This church tolerated no false teaching or false doctrine. Its firm position caused other people to see the error of their ways and to begin worshiping God.

> **Indeed I will make those of the synagogue of Satan, who say they are Jews and are not, but lie — indeed I will make them come and worship before your feet, and to know that I have loved you** (v. 9).

---

[1]Isaiah 35:8; Luke 2:42-48; Proverbs 22:6.

Christians Will Escape the Tribulation

The following Scripture contains two key words:

> **Because you have kept My command to persevere, I also will keep you *from* the hour of *trial* which shall come upon the whole world, to test those who dwell on the earth (v. 10).**

The word *from* makes it clear that those who adhere to the Word will have no part of the hour of temptation, the Tribulation Period.

The people who hold the erroneous view that the Church will go through the Tribulation state that the Church isn't ready to meet the Lord. They interpret "the Church" to be the institutional, man-made religious orders which never will be ready for Jesus. The true Church — consisting wholly of born-again, Spirit-led followers of Jesus who believe in and keep God's Word — will not go through the Tribulation.

The Greek word for *from* in verse 10 is *ek* which means "out of" or "from."[2] Jesus was saying, "Because you have kept My Word with great patience, you will have no part of this hour of Tribulation."

The second key word is *hour*. The meaning of the Greek word for *hour* in this verse indicates far more than a sixty-minute period of time. It refers to an extended period. Both Daniel and Revelation establish that the Tribulation covers seven years.

The Church will not be tried during this period because it is already undergoing trials. It is exercising a tremendous amount of faith to prepare for Jesus' appearing.

Paul says, **For if we would judge ourselves, we would not be judged** (1 Cor. 11:31). The standard we use to judge

---

[2]Robert Young, LL.D., *Analytical Concordance to the Bible*, 22nd ed. (Grand Rapids: William B. Eerdmans, 1964, 1969, 1970), pp. 375,376.

ourselves is God's Word. **For the word of God is living and powerful, and sharper than any two-edged sword...and is a discerner of the thoughts and intents of the heart** (Heb. 4:12). The word *discerner* is also translated "judge."[3] The Word of God is a judge of the intent of the heart.

The apostle Peter says, **The time has come for judgment to begin at the house of God** (1 Pet. 4:17). Our just God judges us, His children, by having us judge ourselves daily with the Word. God has a perfect plan for us. If we abide by it, we will see the desired results reflected in our lives.

If the Tribulation, coming to try them that dwell upon the earth, is designed for the perfection of the saints, it violates the teachings of the apostle Paul. Paul states, **And He Himself** (Jesus) **gave some** (the Church), **to be apostles, some prophets, some evangelists, and some pastors and teachers, for the equipping of the saints for the work of ministry** (Eph. 4:11,12). Paul says the ministry, not the Tribulation, perfects the saints. (See vv. 12-16.)

Paul also reveals that the Lord will present **to Himself a glorious church, not having spot or wrinkle or any such thing, but that she should be holy and without blemish** (Eph. 5:27).

We can easily see that it is by ministry that the Church will become glorious, spiritually mature and ready to be caught up to meet the Lord in the air. No amount of tribulation or persecution could produce such an accomplishment. Revelation (especially Rev. 3:10), the teachings of Jesus and the writings of the apostle Paul clearly teach that the true Church will be caught up before the Tribulation Period begins.

The Lord continues to admonish the Philadelphian church: **Behold, I am coming quickly! Hold fast what you**

---

[3]Ibid., p. 257.

have, that no one may take your crown (v. 11). Jesus admonishes them to stand steadfastly upon what they have learned and heard, to stay in that position based on the Word of God and the name of Jesus.

Verses 12 and 13 contain the statement to the overcomer and the direction to be sensitive to the Holy Spirit:

He who overcomes, I will make him a pillar in the temple of My God, and he shall go out no more. I will write on him the name of My God and the name of the city of My God, the New Jerusalem, which comes down out of heaven from My God. And I will write on him My new name.

He who has an ear, let him hear what the Spirit says to the churches.

The Church of Laodicea

And to the angel of the church of the Laodiceans write, "These things says the Amen, the Faithful and True Witness, the Beginning of the creation of God:

"I know your works, that you are neither cold nor hot. I could wish you were cold or hot. So then, because you are lukewarm, and neither cold nor hot, I will vomit you out of My mouth" (vv. 14-16).

Someone who is red-hot for the Lord walks with Him and is sensitive to Him. Even if he makes a mistake, he is close enough to God to receive instruction and help for correction. He steadily progresses forward. Someone who is cold is usually honest enough to admit that he is out of fellowship with God.

Because of the person's self-righteousness, the Lord will spew out of His mouth someone who is lukewarm. He attempts to convince others that he is as close to God as anyone else and tries to justify his lack of spirituality.

Because you say, "I am rich, and have become wealthy, and have need of nothing" — and do not know that you are wretched, miserable, poor, blind,

**and naked — I counsel you to buy from Me gold refined
in the fire, that you may be rich; and white garments,
that you may be clothed, that the shame of your
nakedness may not be revealed; and anoint your eyes
with eye salve, that you may see** (vv. 17,18).

Jesus tells the Laodicean church, which is rich with
goods having need of nothing, "You are wretched,
miserable, blind and naked. You need to change." When
they fail to become hot, Jesus has no prerogative but to
literally vomit (**spew** KJV) them out.

In the next verse we find out why Jesus takes this
position: **As many as I love, I rebuke and chasten.
Therefore be zealous and repent** (v. 19).

The Lord deals firmly with the Laodiceans because He
loves them. He calls upon them to be zealous and repent,
not to be stubborn. When the Holy Spirit jars you in order
to get your attention, recognize that He is doing it because
He loves you. React in the way He asks.

**Behold, I stand at the door and knock. If anyone
hears My voice and opens the door, I will come in to
him, and dine with him, and he with Me** (v. 20).

Using this Scripture to preach salvation to sinners is
taking it out of context. Occasionally, a text used improperly
still gets results. Verse 20 has drawn many people back to
Jesus or to Him for the first time.

In context, this verse pictures the Lord Jesus outside the
Laodicean church having to knock on the door for an opening
to go inside where He belongs. He should have always been
more than welcome and never forced out. This letter was not
written to the unsaved, but to a lukewarm church.

Verses 21 and 22 contain the statement to the overcomer
and the urging to be sensitive to the Holy Spirit:

**To him who overcomes I will grant to sit with Me
on My throne, as I also overcame and sat down with My
Father on His throne.**

> **He who has an ear, let him hear what the Spirit says to the churches.**

All Scripture Is Profitable

Some theologians teach that only the letter to the Laodiceans holds a message for us today. The apostle Paul taught, **All Scripture is given by inspiration of God (Every Scripture is God-breathed** AMP**), and is profitable...** (2 Tim. 3:16). Every Scripture from Genesis 1:1 to Revelation 22:21 is profitable.

Paul lists the areas in which all Scripture is profitable: **...for doctrine, for reproof, for correction, for instruction in righteousness** (v. 16). We all especially need **instruction in righteousness,** which is right standing with God. We need to study more than our favorite passages — we need the *entire* Word.

Some theologians and ministers explain away the Word of God. They declare that certain things are not for today, having ceased at the end of a certain period or when a certain man died. Translations produced by modern theologians reduce God's Word to being just another book with no chance of changing a person's life. **For I am not ashamed of the gospel of Christ, for it is the power of God to salvation** (Rom. 1:16).

All seven letters to the churches are vitally important to us, because they are the inspired Word of God. Each contains a message for us — either instruction or warnings for us to heed, lest we fall into the same snares as six of the churches.

After recording the seven letters, John's service as secretary to the Lord Jesus is complete. John is now ready for the Holy Spirit and angel of the Lord to impart to him the full body of the prophecy.

PART III
The Prophecy
Revelation 4-9

6

Revelation 4 and 5

Heaven

Chapters 4 and 5 reveal the story unfolding in heaven around God's throne.

> **After these things I looked, and behold, a door standing open in heaven. And the first voice which I heard was like a trumpet speaking with me, saying, "Come up here, and I will show you things which must take place after this."**
>
> **Immediately I was in the Spirit; and behold, a throne set in heaven, and One sat on the throne. And He who sat there was like a jasper and a sardius stone in appearance; and there was a rainbow around the throne, in appearance like an emerald.**
>
> **Revelation 4:1-3**

In Revelation 1 we read that John, when in the Spirit, heard a Voice from behind which sounded like a trumpet. He turned to discover Jesus, from Whom the Voice had come. In Revelation 4:1 we read of a second encounter. Again John hears a Voice which sounds like a trumpet. When it speaks, he is immediately in the Spirit and in heaven at God's throne.

A Parallel of the Rapture

John's prophetic vision is so clear and perfect in detail that God called it "The Revelation of Jesus."

Although John was not taken bodily to heaven in the same manner described in Second Corinthians 12:2, his spiritual experience began with the same event awaiting all believers: a rapture. John's experience parallels the Rapture of the Church described by Paul in First Thessalonians 4:16,17:

> For the Lord Himself will descend from heaven with a shout, with the voice of an archangel, and with the trumpet of God. And the dead in Christ will rise first.
>
> Then we who are alive and remain shall be caught up together with them in the clouds to meet the Lord in the air. And thus we shall always be with the Lord.

John heard a Voice that sounded like a trumpet, then he was taken into heaven. Without question, the Holy Spirit allowed John to experience the Rapture since that event was part of the future. In Scripture, the Rapture is always described as occurring just before the Tribulation.

John's statement, **Immediately I was in the Spirit...in heaven,** harmonizes with Paul's statement, **We shall all be changed — in a moment, in the twinkling of an eye** (1 Cor. 15:51,52). Both depict a swift transition from earth to heaven!

Not only does First Thessalonians 4:16,17 and First Corinthians 15:51,52 harmonize with John's experience in Revelation 4:1-3, but the words of Jesus in Luke 21:36 also agree. Jesus said: **Watch therefore, and pray always that you may be counted worthy to escape all these things that will come to pass, and to stand before the Son of Man.**

Notice that John, according to Revelation 4:1, was *looking*, or watching, and the Voice which he heard commanded him, **Come up here, and I will show you things which must take place after this.** The things he would later witness could only take place after his arrival in heaven, again showing wonderful agreement with Luke 21:36. Furthermore, one must agree that anyone to whom it is commanded, **Come up here,** is going to change locations.

Occasionally some scoffer will criticize those who believe in the catching away of the Church by accusing them of having an "escape mentality." If having such an awareness is wrong, then both Jesus and Paul were mistaken, Jesus in Luke 21:36 and Paul in Hebrews 2:3.

Those of us who are true believers in the catching away of the Church are not sitting idly by, crying for Jesus to hurry and get us out of all our troubles, disappointments, sickness and spiritual setbacks. We know we are more than conquerors, and God has provided *all* that is necessary for life and godliness in this present world. (Rom. 8:37; 2 Pet. 1:3,4.) Therefore, we are constantly overcoming and keeping Satan in a defeated condition.

Because of God's provisions, we do not need Jesus to come and get us out of all these things; but we know He is coming to receive us unto Himself. He has taught us to look for the event, but we must **do business** (NKJV) or **occupy** (KJV) until He comes. (Luke 19:13; 21:28.)

What will we *escape*? First Thessalonians 5:1-11 will explain and answer this question quite well. Notice carefully verses 9-11. It is clear and certain that God may not pour out His wrath until the Church has been removed.[1]

The Personalities of Heaven

Before the throne there was a sea of glass, like crystal. And in the midst of the throne, and around the throne, were four living creatures full of eyes in front and in back.

The first living creature was like a lion, the second living creature like a calf, the third living creature had a face like a man, and the fourth living creature was like a flying eagle.

---

[1]For additional proof, read my book entitled, *Rapture, Get Right or Get Left.*

> The four living creatures, each having six wings, were full of eyes around and within. And they do not rest day or night, saying: "Holy, holy, holy, Lord God Almighty, who was and is and is to come!"
>
> Whenever the living creatures give glory and honor and thanks to Him who sits on the throne, who lives forever and ever, the twenty-four elders fall down before Him who sits on the throne and worship Him who lives forever and ever, and cast their crowns before the throne, saying:
>
> "You are worthy, O Lord, to receive glory and honor and power; for You created all things, and by Your will they exist and were created."
>
> **Revelation 4:6-11**

John describes the personalities in heaven and their activities. He sees God on His throne surrounded by a magnificent rainbow (Rev. 4:3), a reminder of God's covenant with Noah following the Flood. (Gen. 9:13.)

God occasionally shares His glory with His people. After a trying experience with the children of Israel, Moses asked God to show him His glory. (Ex. 33:18.) God answered:

> But He said, "You cannot see My face; for no man shall see Me, and live."
>
> And the Lord said, "Here is a place by Me, and you shall stand on the rock. So it shall be, while My glory passes by, that I will put you in the cleft of the rock, and will cover you with My hand while I pass by. Then I will take away My hand, and you shall see My back; but My face shall not be seen."
>
> **Exodus 33:20-23**

Moses could not have looked upon the glory of God's face and remained alive. At the appearing of Jesus, we will experience a change to glorified bodies. Until then, the glory of God is within us. For the believer today, glory is a state of being. (John 17:22.)

The Elders

Around the throne were twenty-four thrones, and on the thrones I saw twenty-four elders sitting, clothed in white robes; and they had crowns of gold on their heads.

Revelation 4:4

An *elder* is a person God chooses to represent Him and minister to the saints. Jesus shares His ministry with those whom the apostle Paul identifies as "gifts": apostles, prophets, evangelists, pastors and teachers. (Eph. 4:8,11.) In other references, the word *elder* appears, identifying these same "gifts."

From the Old Testament and the book of Revelation, we pick up two additional terms, *olive tree* and *lampstand,* which are symbolic of the character and life of those who are called into the ministry. An olive tree has long life and always produces fruit; a lampstand holds a light which dispels the dark.

Revelation 4 and 5 describe the twenty-four elders in detail. The number *twenty-four* is the double twelve of God's Word. In the Old Testament, twelve is the number of tribes of Israel; in the New Testament, twelve is the number of Jesus' apostles.

The Old Testament saints became part of the dead in Christ through Jesus' death and resurrection. Paul teaches us that when Jesus rose He transferred paradise — a compartment of Sheol ("the place of the dead") in the bowels of the earth — into the presence of God. (Eph. 4:8-10.) Paul wrote that being absent from the body is to be present with the Lord. (2 Cor. 5:8.)

When a child of God dies, he goes immediately into the presence of the Lord in paradise. It is only his physical remains that are placed in the grave. At Jesus' appearing, the dead in Christ, from both the Old and New Testament periods, will be resurrected. We that are alive and remain will be caught up with them in the clouds to meet the Lord in the air. The twenty-four elders represent the entire Church in heaven.

The Holy Spirit

> **And from the throne proceeded lightnings, thunderings, and voices. Seven lamps of fire were burning before the throne, which are the seven Spirits of God.**
>
> **Revelation 4:5**

In heaven John also saw the Holy Spirit, symbolized by the seven spirits of God. There is only one Spirit of God, but He has many manifestations, diversities and operations. The number *seven* refers to God's completion, the perfect operation of the Holy Spirit.

Isaiah 11:2 gives insight into the sevenfold Spirit of God. He is referred to as the Spirit of the Lord; the spirit of wisdom, understanding, counsel, might, knowledge and the fear of the Lord.[2]

The Holy Spirit's presence before the throne of God indicates that He has completed His earthly assignments in behalf of the Church begun on the Jewish feast day of Pentecost.

The Crystal Sea

John sees the crystal sea before the throne. This is not a body of water or large expanse of clear glass. In Scripture a description of a mass of people accompanies the word *sea* whenever it is used without reference to the name or location of an existing body of water.

---

[2]In attempting to interpret Revelation, many people place too much emphasis on numerology. The apostle Paul exhorted us to study the Word of God, not to study numerology, pyramidology or symbolisms.

The crystal sea is a great company of people standing before the throne of God. They are referred to as a *sea* because of their vast numbers and as *crystal* because of their right standing before God. Since the twenty-four elders are representatives, the Church whom they represent must also be in heaven. Thus the crystal sea before the throne is the symbol of the whole Church company in heaven.

Crystal is the only earthly substance in which flaws cannot be hidden; in fact, any flaws are magnified. The Lord will present to Himself **a glorious church, not having spot or wrinkle or any such thing, but...be holy and without blemish** (Eph. 5:27).

Second Peter 2:9-19 describes the spots and blemishes within the Church as those people who focus attention on themselves by declaring how spiritual they are. They attempt to develop a small following by deceiving new Christians who have little or no foundation in the Word.

Revelation 15:2 describes the crystal sea as being **mingled with fire**. This indicates strongly that the Holy Spirit (often symbolized by fire) has produced the crystal sea and is responsible for its presence at the throne of God.

Everything about crystal speaks of the glorious Church: not only its ability to expose flaws, but its beauty, fire and even its melodious sound (made when gently thumped).

Four Great Beasts

John sees four living creatures (**beasts** KJV) before the throne of God. (Rev. 4:8.) The first creature appears like a lion; the second, like a calf; the third has the face of a man; and the fourth is like a flying eagle. The Scripture doesn't explain why the beasts appear in this manner. This is one of the unknowns of Revelation. (See Appendix 1.)

Overly concerned with symbols, some people attempt to squeeze every possible meaning out of each word and often enter into speculation. Failing to brand their thoughts as personal speculation, they present them as "Thus saith the Lord...." We have a right to speculate, but we do not have a right to state our speculations as if said by the Lord. This fosters confusion and disagreement, because many people believe these speculations to be exact.

Why these four creatures appear as they do is only the first of a number of unknowns in Revelation. We will have to wait to find out the meaning of the unknowns.

The creatures play three major roles. First, full of eyes and each having six wings, they are guardians to the throne of God. No one can approach the throne from any direction without being detected by one of them. Second, as angels, they are messengers who assist John with the prophecy. Third, they are God's cheerleaders! Every time they start to say, **Holy, holy, holy, Lord God Almighty, who was and is and is to come,** all who are around the throne prostrate themselves to worship God.

We can see that worship in heaven will be done in divine order because it begins at the signal of the four creatures. In heaven we will enter into a beautiful dimension of worship greater than any we have ever known.

The Reason God Created You

...for You created all things, and by Your will they exist and were created (Rev. 4:11). The *King James Version* says: **...for thou hast created all things, and for thy pleasure they are and were created.**

We exist for the purpose of bringing God great pleasure. Enoch's testimony was that he pleased God: **And Enoch walked with God; and he was not, for God took him** (Gen. 5:24). Today everyone who is pleasing God will be presented before His throne!

Jesus and the Church

And I saw in the right hand of Him who sat on the throne a scroll written inside and on the back, sealed with seven seals.

Then I saw a strong angel proclaiming with a loud voice, "Who is worthy to open the scroll and to loose its seals?"

And no one in heaven or on the earth or under the earth was able to open the scroll, or to look at it. So I wept much, because no one was found worthy to open and read the scroll, or to look at it.

But one of the elders said to me, "Do not weep. Behold, the Lion of the tribe of Judah, the Root of David, has prevailed to open the scroll and to loose its seven seals."

And I looked, and behold, in the midst of the throne and of the four living creatures, and in the midst of the elders, stood a Lamb as though it had been slain, having seven horns and seven eyes, which are the seven Spirits of God sent out into all the earth.

Revelation 5:1-6

Revelation 5 continues John's description of heaven. He beholds Jesus *standing* at the throne before His Father. Presently Jesus is seated in His Father's throne.

Following His ascension back to heaven, Jesus sat down on the right hand of the Father where He serves as High Priest, making daily intercession for us. (Heb. 8:1; Rom. 8:34.) This gives us the most complete representation possible before the throne. In exchange, Jesus simply asks us to represent Him on earth. The Holy Spirit empowers believers daily to do this. We should do our utmost for Him, representing Him in the best possible way.

Many believers are succeeding as capable witnesses. The world will know that Jesus Christ is indeed the Son of God because they will see His followers working, praying and pulling together. All divisions, feuds and "splitting of hairs" over minor theological viewpoints will fade away as the love of Christ perfects us all. (See John 17.)

John pictures Jesus standing, not sitting. Jesus had just left the throne of God to quickly appear above the earth to receive the true Church unto Himself. Together the whole company proceeded to the throne of God. Having just returned, Jesus is standing with His company among the elders.

After Jesus walks back to the throne and takes a scroll from the hand of God, He is ready to begin opening the seals of the scroll.

Verse 6 depicts the perfectly harmonious relationship between Jesus Christ the Lamb, and the Holy Spirit. Jesus describes that relationship in the following passage:

> But when the Helper comes, whom I shall send to you from the Father, the Spirit of truth who proceeds from the Father, He will testify of Me. And you also will bear witness, because you have been with Me from the beginning.
>
> **John 15:26,27**

The seven horns and seven eyes of the Lamb symbolize the seven Spirits of God sent to the earth.

Revelation 5 continues:

> Then He came and took the scroll out of the right hand of Him who sat on the throne.
>
> Now when He had taken the scroll, the four living creatures and the twenty-four elders fell down before the Lamb, each having a harp, and golden bowls full of incense, which are the prayers of the saints.
>
> And they sang a new song, saying: "You are worthy to take the scroll, and to open its seals; for You were slain, and have redeemed us to God by Your blood out of every tribe and tongue and people and nation, and

have made us kings and priests to our God; and we shall reign on the earth."

Then I looked, and I heard the voice of many angels around the throne, the living creatures, and the elders; and the number of them was ten thousand times ten thousand, and thousands of thousands, saying with a loud voice: "Worthy is the Lamb who was slain to receive power and riches and wisdom, and strength and honor and glory and blessing!"

And every creature which is in heaven and on the earth and under the earth and such as are in the sea, and all that are in them, I heard saying: "Blessing and honor and glory and power be to Him who sits on the throne, and to the Lamb, forever and ever!"

Then the four living creatures said, "Amen!" And the twenty-four elders fell down and worshiped Him who lives forever and ever.

Revelation 5:7-14

Everything written about the twenty-four elders also applies to all practicing believers.

In Revelation 4:4 the elders are described as having "thrones." The Word teaches, **...we shall reign on the earth** (Rev. 5:10).

The elders wore white robes (**raiment** KJV) and **crowns of gold** (Rev. 4:4).

Revelation 5 tells us that the elders are associated with the prayers of saints. (v. 8.) They sing **a new song** (v. 9) that they have been redeemed by the blood of the Lamb from all nations. This clearly identifies them as earthlings.

John sees the representatives of the Church before the throne of God as Jesus opens the first seal. When the Tribulation begins, the Church company is standing in heaven to observe the results.

The Angels

John sees the angelic company comprised of **ten thousand times ten thousand, and thousands of**

thousands (v. 11) — 100 billion! The doctrine of guardian angels, who also minister, is biblical.

Angels are assigned to minister to and for every born-again child of God. Paul says, **Are they** (the angels) **not all ministering spirits sent forth to minister for those who will inherit salvation?** (Heb. 1:14).

God's angels watch over you constantly to protect you. **For He** (the Lord) **shall give His angels charge over you, to keep you in all your ways. In their hands they shall bear you up, lest you dash your foot against a stone** (Ps. 91:11,12).

It is possible to entertain an angel and be unaware of it. (See Heb. 13:2.) The saints have a tremendous work to accomplish in these end times. Do not be distracted by looking for angels (or hunting for demons). Just realize that God has approximately 100 billion angels to assist in behalf of the Church!

The presence of the angelic host before the throne of God is further proof that the Church has been caught up to heaven. Angels are on divine assignment in behalf of the righteous on earth. If the Church were still on earth, the angels would not be in heaven.

Summary

Surrounding God, John has seen a great rainbow, the twenty-four elders who represent the crystal sea (the Church), and the Holy Spirit. Like the Father and Son, the Holy Spirit resides both in heaven on the throne and within each believer. His priority assignment, however, is an earthly one. In the scene John describes, the Holy Spirit, having completed one phase of His assignment concerning the Church, stands with Jesus and the Church before God's throne.

John then describes the crystal sea, the four living creatures (God's cheerleaders), Jesus Christ the Lamb, and, lastly, the angelic company.

Amazing as it may seem, Paul summarized Revelation, chapters 4 and 5, when he wrote:

> **But you have come to Mount Zion and to the city of the living God, the heavenly Jerusalem, to an innumerable company of angels, to the general assembly and church of the firstborn who are registered in heaven, to God the Judge of all, to the spirits of just men made perfect, to Jesus the Mediator of the new covenant, and to the blood of sprinkling that speaks better things than that of Abel.**
>
> **Hebrews 12:22-24**

Paul speaks of the city of the living God, Mount Zion, the heavenly Jerusalem; of 100 billion angels; of the general assembly of the Church — the firstborn registered in heaven; of God the Judge and Jesus the Mediator. Paul and John are in agreement. They place the Church in heaven, not on the earth. A catching away of the Church is assured; there is too much Scripture to doubt it.

7

Revelation 6
Earth

In Revelation 6 we read that Jesus stands before the throne and opens six of the seven seals of the scroll He has taken from His Father's hand.

> Now I saw when the Lamb opened one of the seals; and I heard one of the four living creatures saying with a voice like thunder, "Come and see." And I looked, and behold, a white horse. He who sat on it had a bow; and a crown was given to him, and he went out conquering and to conquer.
>
> When He opened the second seal, I heard the second living creature saying, "Come and see." Another horse, fiery red, went out. And it was granted to the one who sat on it to take peace from the earth, and that people should kill one another; and there was given to him a great sword.
>
> When He opened the third seal, I heard the third living creature say, "Come and see." So I looked, and behold, a black horse, and he who sat on it had a pair of scales in his hand.
>
> And I heard a voice in the midst of the four living creatures saying, "A quart of wheat for a denarius, and three quarts of barley for a denarius; and do not harm the oil and the wine."
>
> When He opened the fourth seal, I heard the voice of the fourth living creature saying, "Come and see." So I looked, and behold, a pale horse. And the name of him who sat on it was Death, and Hades followed with

him. **And power was given to them over a fourth of the earth, to kill with sword, with hunger, with death, and by the beasts of the earth** (vv. 1-8).

In heaven Jesus opens the first seal shortly after the Church is taken up, possibly on the same day. From this point the activities of the earthly story unfold. Notice that the four living creatures (**four beasts** KJV), of a special angelic order, assist John with understanding.

The Antichrist Released

The first four seals release the horsemen often referred to as "the four horsemen of the Apocalypse." They ride throughout the entire Tribulation Period.

The opening of the first seal releases the white horse with a rider. Formerly, many religious leaders and writers identified this rider as Jesus because Revelation 19:11 describes Jesus as riding a white horse. Some have reasoned that the appearing of Jesus and the Rapture will cause great confusion and crisis upon earth. They believe Jesus will, in turn, come to earth to conduct a great seven-year revival. During this time Jesus will be at work, but not in that way.

The rider of the white horse referred to in Revelation 6 has a bow but no arrows. A bow and arrow constitutes a lethal weapon. Having been stripped of his armor (Luke 11:21,22), Satan could only supply a bow. This also indicates further deception. We know that the white horse rider has no crown, because one has to be given to him. (v. 2.) He has not yet conquered, because **...he went out conquering and to conquer** (v. 2).

The Scriptures always describe Jesus as using the two-edged Sword (the Word of God), never a bow and arrow. Jesus has many crowns. (Rev. 19:12.) After He defeated Satan — rising victoriously over death, hell and the grave — He testified, **All authority has been given to Me in heaven and on earth** (Matt. 28:18). He demonstrated His victory for forty magnificent days. Jesus is certainly a conqueror!

The rider of Revelation 6:2 is the man destined to become the Antichrist. During the first three-and-one-half years of his term, he is not identified as the Antichrist, but as a great world diplomat.

Although the Bible hides the Antichrist's personal identity (the second unknown of Revelation), it reveals other things about him. We know his nature, his characteristics and the source of his power and authority. We know his plan, the way in which he will attempt to carry it out, and the end results. Rather than trying to identify the Antichrist, watch for the system that produces him. (Rev. 13 and 17 vividly describe that system.)

Both Revelation 6:1,2 and Daniel 9:24-27 teach that the opening of the first seal releases the Antichrist to begin his satanic assignment. Daniel states that at the beginning of the week, or the seven-year Tribulation Period, the Antichrist enters into an agreement with Israel. Supported by nations within a vast European-Mediterranean system, he is attempting to propel himself into the position of world dictator. Because Israel has just conquered Russia, the Antichrist needs Israel's favor to increase in power. But after three-and-one-half years, in mid-Tribulation, he breaks his agreement with Israel.

Paul's teachings recorded in Second Thessalonians 2:1-9 harmonize with those of Revelation and Daniel. Paul teaches that the man of sin cannot be revealed to begin his activity until that which hinders (**restrains** v. 7 NKJV) him is taken out of the way. Today on earth, the true Church energized by the Holy Ghost holds back Satan's best plan. Once the true Church is caught up to meet Jesus when He appears in the air, the last remaining hindrance to Satan's plan is removed. Then the Antichrist comes forth quickly.

As the pieces continue to fit together, we see further confirmation that at the beginning of the Tribulation Period, when Jesus opens the first seal, the true Church is already before God's throne.

Some prophecy teachers teach that the "withholder" (**what is restraining** v. 6 NKJV) of Satan's plan, as revealed in Second Thessalonians 2, is the Holy Spirit. Based on such teaching, the Holy Spirit would be removed at the beginning of the seven-year Tribulation Period.

Please observe the prophecy of Joel, chapter 2, reiterated by the apostle Peter in Acts, chapter 2, beginning with verse 16. Both the prophet and the apostle agree that once the Holy Spirit begins being poured out, the outpouring continues until the day the sun becomes black and the moon as blood. According to Jesus in Matthew 24:29, this event affecting the sun and moon occurs at the end of the Tribulation. Joel 2:28-31 supports this statement made by Jesus. We know by the prophecy of Joel, the statement of Jesus and the teaching of Peter in Acts 2 that the Holy Spirit is here throughout the seven years of Tribulation.

Since the Holy Spirit is not removed so the Antichrist can be revealed, who is the "withholder" that must be removed?

There can be only one choice: the true Church, that company of born-again followers of Jesus. This company, called *the Church*, is also identified by the apostle Paul as *the Body of Christ*. One can only conclude, according to Second Thessalonians 2:1-12, that the Church must be caught away so that the Antichrist can be revealed. This is the second biblical reason for the removal of the Church. The first one is found in First Thessalonians 5:9,10.

The Man of War

The opening of the second seal releases a rider on a red horse — the man of war given power to take peace from the earth. His release clearly establishes that war will take place during the Tribulation.

The man's first action is to disrupt the peace between Israel and her Arab neighbors by sending Russia from the north. This fulfills prophecy in Ezekiel 38. Ezekiel places this battle, which brings about the total destruction of Russia, at the beginning of the Tribulation.

Russia's destruction removes a major opposition to the Antichrist. Because the world has been without true peace for generations, the stage is set for the Antichrist's attempt to carry out his commission from Satan to conquer the world. (Rev. 13:2,7.)

Incidentally, the Russian Christians will have escaped destruction by reason of the Rapture. They have as much right as other Christians to these words of Jesus: **Watch therefore, and pray always that you may be counted worthy to escape all these things that will come to pass, and to stand before the Son of Man** (Luke 21:36).

Many Christians believe that under the Antichrist — a pseudo-man of peace — there is no war. However, we have discovered that the Antichrist has a man of war at his disposal: the rider of the red horse. The Antichrist is a man of destruction but is known as a man of peace strictly because of his ability to deceive. In an insurrection against him, the Antichrist destroys three of the original ten nations which support him. (Dan. 7:8,24.) His followers say he destroys wonderfully. By peace he destroys many. (Dan. 8:24,25; see also Dan. 11:21,24.)

All attempts made by evil men to conquer the world have failed. The Antichrist will also fail. Jesus is the only Man Who will ever rule the world and bring peace.

Research world history from biblical times until now and discover how many different men have attempted to conquer the world. All were ungodly and failed miserably.

Satan himself cannot take the earth from God, so he keeps looking for the right human, one whom he can use to attempt this theft. (Ps. 24:1.)

Famine

The opening of the third seal releases the black horse and rider: famine. Famine does not mean there is no food, but a serious shortage of food during the Tribulation. Such conditions are always the results of tremendous upheavals of nature and protracted wars.

Although there is widespread famine in the European-Mediterranean area, no worldwide famine is prophesied.

We know that during the Tribulation some nations will still have food because the remnant of Israel is hidden in an area with an ample food supply. (Rev. 12:14.)

Death

The opening of the fourth seal releases the pale horse whose rider is Death. With him rides an evil companion: *Hades* **followed with him** (Rev. 6:8). Over a seven-year period these horsemen destroy one-fourth of the earth's remaining population. No wonder the Scripture says that hell enlarges itself. (Isa. 5:14.) A great number of people unprepared to meet God will be destroyed during the Tribulation.

The Tribulation Martyrs

The opening of the fifth seal reveals the martyrs of the Tribulation.

> **When He opened the fifth seal, I saw under the altar the souls of those who had been slain for the word of God and for the testimony which they held.**
>
> **And they cried with a loud voice, saying, "How long, O Lord, holy and true, until You judge and avenge our blood on those who dwell on the earth?"**

Then a white robe was given to each of them; and it was said to them that they should rest a little while longer, until both the number of their fellow servants and their brethren, who would be killed as they were, was completed (vv. 9-11).

These martyrs are not part of the Church Age which has already ended with Jesus' appearing and the catching up of the Church. Here is our first evidence that many people will be saved during the Tribulation.

The teaching that martyrdom is the only way for someone who misses the Rapture to be saved during the Tribulation is erroneous. Paul says, **Though I bestow all my goods to feed the poor, and though I give my body to be burned, but have not love, it profits me nothing** (1 Cor. 13:3).

There is no salvation in becoming a martyr, even when doing it in the name of the Lord. Only a small number of the group saved during the Tribulation face martyrdom. Those saved during the first three-and-one-half years are not as apt to be martyred as those who are saved in the second half of the Tribulation. However, those who are martyred will cry out for vengeance.

God tells them to stay at rest under the great altar before His throne until their company becomes complete. At that time He will avenge all of them at once. When the Two Witnesses, serving in Jerusalem for three-and-one-half years, have been put to death by the Antichrist, the company of martyrs will be complete. The Two Witnesses are slain four days before the end of the Tribulation. The martyrs are avenged by Armageddon and resurrected to reign with Christ on earth.

Nature's Upheaval

The opening of the sixth seal releases a tremendous upheaval of nature.

> I looked when He opened the sixth seal, and behold, there was a great earthquake; and the sun became black as sackcloth of hair, and the moon became like blood. And the stars of heaven fell to the earth, as a fig tree drops its late figs when it is shaken by a mighty wind.
>
> Then the sky receded as a scroll when it is rolled up, and every mountain and island was moved out of its place.
>
> And the kings of the earth, the great men, the rich men, the commanders, the mighty men, every slave and every free man, hid themselves in the caves and in the rocks of the mountains, and said to the mountains and rocks, "Fall on us and hide us from the face of Him who sits on the throne and from the wrath of the Lamb" (vv. 12-16).

There is a great earthquake; the sun becomes black as sackcloth of hair, the moon red as blood; and the stars of heaven fall. The upheaval affects even the mountains and islands.

All people on earth are able to see the Father, sitting on the throne, and the Lamb. The wrath of the Lamb falls: **For the great day of His wrath has come, and who is able to stand?** (v. 17).

The rapid and progressive development of technology, as prophesied in Daniel 12:4, has placed the Hubble Space Telescope in the heavens. Now that this telescope is operating at full power, man has the ability to peer fourteen billion lightyears into space.

Without such a powerful instrument, man with his natural sight could not see that far. The eye is an absolutely marvelous part of the body, but an airplane can fly out of our sight range in only a couple of minutes.

The Hubble Space Telescope connected to downlinks and television will allow men to see into heaven once the sky is rolled back. Isaiah 34:4 and Revelation 6:14 reveal the sky to be tangible; therefore, it can be rolled up as a scroll. Once the sky is rolled up, or parted, heaven is visible. Men will know by the expression on God's face that they are in trouble and will be running for a hiding place.

In Matthew 24:29 we read another description of the same event:

> **Immediately after the tribulation of those days the sun will be darkened, and the moon will not give its light; the stars will fall from heaven, and the powers of the heavens will be shaken.**

Jesus made the above statement in response to His disciples' question, **What will be the sign of Your coming, and of the end of the age?** (Matt. 24:3).

The upheaval occurs on the final, and worst, day of the Tribulation Period. Jesus departs heaven, returns to earth and stands on the Mount of Olives, beginning His activities. The armies of the Antichrist are destroyed in the Battle of Armageddon. Jesus conquers the governments on the earth and begins His 1,000-year reign of peace.

Notice that these events occur when Jesus returns in His wrath to conquer and rule the world, not when He appears to receive the Church. The results of the opening of this seal are reserved for the final day of Tribulation.

8

Revelation 7
Informational

Revelation 7 interrupts the story of the events taking place on earth to inform us of God's activities. Contrary to what some people think, God does not turn the seven years over to Satan and the Antichrist. During this time, God performs in all His greatness.

At the start of the Tribulation, the Church is caught up. God in His mercy creates a powerful vehicle to replace it. One hundred forty-four thousand Jewish evangelists, introduced in Revelation 7, begin their ministry. God gives Israel a great victory over Russia in one day. (Ezek. 38.) This removes the temporary blindness from the Israelis' eyes, again restoring them to the God of Abraham.

Taking over the assignment of the Church, the 144,000 preach the Gospel. A seal of God provides them with divine immunity, causing their ministry to be so effective that a great multitude of people is converted to Jesus. When God translates those converts into His presence, He spares them from the wrath of the Antichrist at mid-Tribulation.

The 144,000 Jewish Evangelists

After these things I saw four angels standing at the four corners of the earth, holding the four winds of the earth, that the wind should not blow on the earth, on the sea, or on any tree.

Then I saw another angel ascending from the east, having the seal of the living God. And he cried with a loud voice to the four angels to whom it was granted to harm the earth and the sea, saying, "Do not harm the earth, the sea, or the trees till we have sealed the servants of our God on their foreheads" (vv. 1-3).

Reflecting godly order, the angel of verse 2 verbally restrains the four angels of Revelation 8 from releasing plagues upon the earth and stars until after the 144,000 are sealed.

The 144,000 are identified as "servants of God." One serves God by carrying out a divine assignment. Obedience is a characteristic of a servant of God. Disobedience certainly does not serve God or man. The effective ministry of the 144,000 is evidence that they preach the Gospel.

Why call them evangelists? Paul writes to Timothy and makes this statement: **But you be watchful in all things, endure afflictions, do the work of an evangelist, fulfill your ministry** (2 Tim. 4:5). One does not have to be called as an evangelist to do the work of one. All believers, including the 144,000, are to carry out the instructions of Jesus in Mark 16:15. Since God's Word never changes, it is the same for believers during the Tribulation as today.

Paul further states plainly that no one can believe and accept Christ unless someone is sent to him:

> **For "whoever calls on the name of the Lord shall be saved."**
> **How then shall they call on Him in whom they have not believed? And how shall they believe in Him of whom they have not heard? And how shall they hear without a preacher?**
> **And how shall they preach unless they are sent? As it is written: "How beautiful are the feet of those who preach the gospel of peace, who bring glad tidings of good things!"**
> **Romans 10:13-15**

According to Romans 11:25,26, **All Israel will be saved.** By using the means described in Romans 10, the 144,000 are to bring all Israel to salvation. In addition, the many Gentiles are saved as well.

> Thus says the Lord of hosts: "In those days ten men from every language of the nations shall grasp the sleeve of a Jewish man, saying, 'Let us go with you, for we have heard that God is with you.'"
>
> Zechariah 8:23

The 144,000 Are Sealed

> And I heard the number of those who were sealed. One hundred and forty-four thousand of all the tribes of the children of Israel were sealed.
>
> Revelation 7:4

John then lists 12,000 sealed of each of the twelve tribes, which totals 144,000. Two of the tribes named are different from those listed in the original twelve of the Old Testament. The tribes of Dan and Ephraim lost their inheritance through idolatry. It is true that all the tribes fell into idolatry, but Dan and Ephraim were more rebellious than any of the others. In their place God substitutes the tribes of Levi (out of which the priesthood comes) and Joseph. The remnants of Dan and Ephraim will eventually be cared for through the goodness of the other tribes.

Revelation 14 completes the description of the 144,000:

> Then I looked, and behold, a Lamb standing on Mount Zion, and with Him one hundred and forty-four thousand, having His Father's name written on their foreheads.
>
> And I heard a voice from heaven, like the voice of many waters, and like the voice of loud thunder. And I heard the sound of harpists playing their harps.
>
> They sang as it were a new song before the throne, before the four living creatures, and the elders; and no one could learn that song except the hundred and forty-four thousand who were redeemed from the earth.

These are the ones who were not defiled with women, for they are virgins. These are the ones who follow the Lamb wherever He goes. These were redeemed from among men, being firstfruits to God and to the Lamb.

And in their mouth was found no deceit, for they are without fault before the throne of God.

Revelation 14:1-5

The 144,000 are redeemed men of the earth. Approximately four years after the Tribulation begins, these servants of God finish their assignment. Revelation 9 shows us that the 144,000 are still on earth just past mid-Tribulation point. After that, they are not mentioned. Jesus meets them at Mount Zion (part of Jerusalem) and immediately escorts them to God's throne. Learning the new song of the redeemed, they join in singing with the Church company. They arrive in time to be part of the great wedding ceremony.

The 144,000 are saved through the ministry of an angel. (See Ezek. 9 and Rev. 7:3.) They gather with weapons to defend Israel and Jerusalem against the great northern power.[1] Following the quick victory, they return to the temple mount. With a writer's inkhorn by his side, the angel selects and seals them from among the crowd.

The 144,000 are the **firstfruits to God and to the Lamb** (v. 4). The word *firstfruits* identifies these Jewish evangelists as being the first to be saved at the beginning of the Tribulation.

Having a tremendous task to perform in a limited amount of time, the 144,000 are unmarried. They must carry the simple Gospel message wherever the people of Israel have been dispersed so that all Israel may be saved.

---

[1]The battle of Ezekiel 9 is contingent upon the restoration of the state of Israel. In Ezekiel's time, Israel was in captivity. She did not exist between 608 B.C. and May, 1948.

Family responsibilities would prevent them from giving themselves totally to their assignment.

These descendants of Abraham are Israel. To say that the Church has taken the place of Israel violates Paul's teachings. Paul distinctly distinguishes between the natural seed of Abraham — the nation of Israel — and the spiritual seed — the Church. (See Rom. 11.)

Paul admonishes the wild olive branch, the spiritual seed, not to boast over having been grafted into the olive tree. God, Who grafted it in, is also able to graft in again the broken-off natural branch, Israel, when she ceases from her unbelief.

The most difficult part of the Tribulation is the second half. During the first half, the man destined to be the Antichrist tries to sell himself as a man of peace. At mid-Tribulation he becomes extremely frustrated with the people of Israel who, except for a small remnant, have given their lives to Jesus. The Antichrist breaks his agreement and turns to destroy them. Some of the converts suffer martyrdom, while most escape the threats of the Antichrist when they are taken to heaven.

The Great Multitude

Revelation 7 describes the mid-Tribulation catching up of the Great Multitude, the converts of the 144,000 Jewish evangelists:

> **After these things I looked, and behold, a great multitude which no one could number, of all nations, tribes, peoples, and tongues, standing before the throne and before the Lamb, clothed with white robes, with palm branches in their hands, and crying out with a loud voice, saying, "Salvation belongs to our God who sits on the throne, and to the Lamb!"**
>
> **All the angels stood around the throne and the elders and the four living creatures, and fell on their**

faces before the throne and worshiped God, saying: "Amen! Blessing and glory and wisdom, thanksgiving and honor and power and might, be to our God forever and ever. Amen."

Then one of the elders answered, saying to me, "Who are these arrayed in white robes, and where did they come from?" And I said to him, "Sir, you know."

So he said to me, "These are the ones who come out of the great tribulation, and washed their robes and made them white in the blood of the Lamb. Therefore they are before the throne of God, and serve Him day and night in His temple. And He who sits on the throne will dwell among them.

"They shall neither hunger anymore nor thirst anymore; the sun shall not strike them, nor any heat; for the Lamb who is in the midst of the throne will shepherd them and lead them to living fountains of waters. And God will wipe away every tear from their eyes" (vv. 9-17).

Before the throne of God, John observes the Great Multitude composed of people from all nations. Basically, they are a Jewish group among a multitude of converted Gentiles. (See Zech. 8:23.) They hold palm leaves; speak of the salvation of their God and the Lamb; and **come out of the great tribulation** (Rev. 7:14), having known much suffering upon the earth. They worship the Lord day and night in His temple and are able to clean their white robes, previously blemished, only by washing them in the blood of the Lamb. Someone had to explain this cleansing and lead them in worship of the Lamb. (Rom. 10:13-15.)

The reference, Revelation 7:9-17, tells us that the Great Multitude is composed of the converts of the 144,000.

Matthew 25 contains the parable of the ten wise and foolish virgins. All the virgins had the same opportunity; all arose when the cry was made, **Behold, the bridegroom is coming** (v. 6). But the lamps of the foolish started going out because they had not brought sufficient oil. The difference between the wise and foolish virgins is that the foolish ones had not kept themselves ready for the event which they knew was coming. While they were gone to prepare themselves, the Bridegroom came. The wise went with Him into the marriage chamber, and the door was shut. (vv. 1-10.)

Backsliders and lukewarm Christians will not be ready for Jesus' appearing; therefore, they will miss the catching up of the Church. Today the Holy Spirit is working so mightily, thousands of Gentile backsliders are daily returning to God. The few believers who miss the Rapture can be caught up with the Great Multitude, provided they too have accepted the ministry of the 144,000 Jewish evangelists.

The company of Revelation 7 differs considerably from the Church company of Revelation 4 and 5. Jesus meets the Church in the air. At the rapture of the Great Multitude, the dead are not resurrected. Once the multitude arrives in heaven, God hides away the remnant of unsaved Israel to prevent its destruction by the Antichrist. The members of the Church have crowns of gold, sit upon thrones and sing the new song. None of this applies to the Great Multitude. The members of the Church declare themselves to be kings and priests reigning with the Lord, whereas those of the Great Multitude identify themselves as both Jews and Gentiles.

Revelation 7 gives us tremendous insight into God's plan for the Jews during the first half of the Tribulation. God continues to keep His Word for both the natural seed of Abraham and Gentile believers.

9

Revelation 8
Earth
Four Plagues Released

Revelation 8 begins with mid-Tribulation, picking up the story of earth from Revelation 6.

Events at Mid-Tribulation

With the events occurring in heaven and on earth during the first half of the Tribulation Period, God's master performance is underway. He has put on quite a show, destroying Russia and sparing Israel. The 144,000 Jewish evangelists are on a worldwide soulwinning crusade. All Israel and hundreds of millions of Gentiles are being saved.

The Antichrist has been busy preparing to make his move toward world conquest by mid-Tribulation. Satan has chosen a talented, resourceful and capable person. Although he began with all the prefabricated components of his vehicle, the Antichrist has had the difficult task of putting them together. Beginning with the support of ten nations, he has had only forty-two months to combine their governments and their commercial, military and religious departments.

At mid-Tribulation, the Antichrist is already badly beaten. Expansion of the satanic empire is becoming difficult; internal problems are critical. Three of the original nations, or horns, have revolted. (According to Dan. 7 the

Antichrist will uproot and replace them with three other nations. We know his effort is successful because ten national armies are following him at the Battle of Armageddon.) Satan is furious and the Antichrist frustrated.

Ten major events occur or begin at mid-Tribulation and cover only a few days. (Dan. 9:27 and Rev. 7:9-17; 11:2,3 establish the time frame for these events.)

1. Antichrist breaks his agreement with Israel. (Dan. 9:27.)

2. Tribulation saints are caught up. (Rev. 7:9-17.)

3. An earthquake occurs. (Rev. 8:5.)

4. Through Antichrist, Satan makes war against Israel; remnant of Israel is hidden away. (Dan. 9; Rev. 12:13-17.)

5. Antichrist destroys religious system. (Rev. 17:16-18.)

6. Antichrist holds press conference from Jerusalem. (2 Thess. 2:4.)

7. False Prophet introduces mark of the Beast. (Rev. 13:16-18.)

8. Two Witnesses begin ministry. (Rev. 11.)

9. Angels begin ministry to all nations. (Rev. 14.)

10. Plagues begin. (Rev. 8,9.)

The Antichrist breaks the agreement he made with Israel at the beginning of the seven years and makes war against her, intending to destroy both the converted Jews and other saints. From this point, activities build toward a mighty crescendo, which takes place on the final day of the Tribulation.

The converts of the 144,000 escape the wrath of Satan and the Antichrist when God briefly delays the invasion with an earthquake.[1] This provides time for Him to simply "snatch" the converts from the Antichrist's path and place them before His throne. At the same time, the yet-unsaved remnant of Israel is whisked into hiding for the next three-and-one-half years.

The Antichrist's armies invade Israel and take over Jerusalem where the Antichrist establishes his head-quarters.

At a worldwide press conference televised via satellite, the Antichrist is seen and heard by all. He introduces the False Prophet, who ushers in the mark of the Beast and idolatry through worship of the Beast's image. Then the Antichrist makes his historical statement: "I am God." (2 Thess. 2:4.)

The Two Witnesses (the prophets of God introduced in Rev. 11), among the observers in Jerusalem, immediately challenge the Antichrist. They use supernatural fire to consume the security men who have surged toward them. Via television, the world has seen that the Antichrist has no power over the two prophets of God.

Angels have begun vocally warning all nations not to receive the mark of the Beast nor worship his image. They also preach the everlasting Gospel. The "new god" has no power over the angels.

The four angels of Revelation 8 sound their trumpets, releasing the plagues of God's wrath. The news media reports the cataclysmic effects of these plagues on the earth, sun, moon and stars. The Antichrist cannot control nature.

The world wonders, *What kind of god is this fellow?* He cannot overcome two men, nor control the angels or nature. These developments further hinder the Antichrist's attempts to carry out his assignment.

---

[1]Although severe, this upheaval of nature is not to be compared with the intensity of the final upheaval of Revelation 6 occurring on the Tribulation's last day.

Earth's Story Continues

As Revelation 8 begins, the scene unfolds in heaven in preparation for the continuation of earthly events. The seventh seal is opened:

> **When he opened the seventh seal, there was silence in heaven for about half an hour (v. 1).**

The half-hour space of silence in heaven is the third unknown of Revelation. The awesomeness of the things about to usher in the last half of the Tribulation Period could inspire the silence. However, any attempt to explain would be speculation. Again we will have to wait and see what this unknown means.

The angels are given their trumpets:

> **And I saw the seven angels who stand before God, and to them were given seven trumpets. Then another angel, having a golden censer, came and stood at the altar. He was given much incense, that he should offer it with the prayers of all the saints upon the golden altar which was before the throne.**
>
> **And the smoke of the incense, with the prayers of the saints, ascended before God from the angel's hand. Then the angel took the censer, filled it with fire from the altar, and threw it to the earth. And there were noises, thunderings, lightnings, and an earthquake (vv. 2-5).**

The first four angels sound their trumpets releasing the plagues:

> **So the seven angels who had the seven trumpets prepared themselves to sound.**
>
> **The first angel sounded: And hail and fire followed, mingled with blood, and they were thrown to the earth. And a third of the trees were burned up, and all green grass was burned up.**
>
> **Then the second angel sounded: And something like a great mountain burning with fire was thrown**

into the sea, and a third of the sea became blood. And a third of the living creatures in the sea died, and a third of the ships were destroyed.

Then the third angel sounded: And a great star fell from heaven, burning like a torch, and it fell on a third of the rivers and on the springs of water. The name of the star is Wormwood. A third of the waters became wormwood, and many men died from the water, because it was made bitter.

Then the fourth angel sounded: And a third of the sun was struck, a third of the moon, and a third of the stars, so that a third of them were darkened. A third of the day did not shine, and likewise the night.

And I looked, and I heard an angel flying through the midst of heaven, saying with a loud voice, "Woe, woe, woe to the inhabitants of the earth, because of the remaining blasts of the trumpet of the three angels who are about to sound!" (vv. 6-13).

The plagues are controlled by the Two Witnesses who use them against the Antichrist throughout the last half of the Tribulation as they deem it necessary.

With the sounding of the first trumpet comes fire and hail mingled with blood. This kind of rain falls in many places during the last half of the Tribulation destroying green grass and one-third of the trees.[2] Many homes and commercial buildings will also be destroyed by reason of this plague.

When the second trumpet sounds, a third of the oceans (sea v. 8) become blood in the European-Mediterranean area. Ships caught, sink; and all aboard perish. By the end of the Two Witnesses' ministry, even people living inland will be affected as waters are turned into blood.

---

[2]There will also be natural rain. From reading Revelation 12:14 we know that the area where the Israeli remnant is hidden is free from the effects of the plagues. Since the plagues controlled by the Two Witnesses are not worldwide, natural rain will also continue.

When the third trumpet sounds, a great star falls, poisoning one-third of the sources of domestic waters. Those people who drink from these waters die. This could destroy entire cities.

When the fourth trumpet sounds, a third of the moon, sun and stars are immediately darkened. They give no light for one-third of the day and night.

During the Tribulation, the major form of religion will be witchcraft, which involves astrology. The already alarming increase in today's use of witchcraft is only a forerunner of what will come. The sudden plague upon the heavenly bodies will place astrologers in a state of confusion and drastically affect those people who look to astrology for guidance, placing them in an even worse state of confusion.

Verse 13 warns that there are three woes to come, each worse than any of the plagues released by the sounding of the first four trumpets.

10
Revelation 9
Earth
Fifth and Sixth Woes Released

The Plague of Locusts

At the sound of the fifth trumpet, a plague of demon-controlled locusts begins.

> Then the fifth angel sounded: And I saw a star fallen from heaven to the earth. To him was given the key to the bottomless pit. And he opened the bottomless pit, and smoke arose out of the pit like the smoke of a great furnace. So the sun and the air were darkened because of the smoke of the pit. Then out of the smoke locusts came upon the earth. And to them was given power, as the scorpions of the earth have power.
>
> They were commanded not to harm the grass of the earth, or any green thing, or any tree, but only those men who do not have the seal of God on their foreheads. And they were not given authority to kill them, but to torment them for five months. Their torment was like the torment of a scorpion when it strikes a man (vv. 1-5).

The locusts are commanded not to harm the grass of the earth. We know that the first plague has not run its course, or there would be no grass for the locusts to hurt. Since the locusts are instructed to hurt only the men who do not have the seal of God on their foreheads, we know that the 144,000 are still on the earth ministering after mid-

Tribulation. (Approximately six months later, they are met by Jesus at Mount Zion and taken up to God's throne.)

Beginning shortly after mid-Tribulation, this plague covers a five-month period and is not repeated. During this time the remnant of Israel, who has not yet accepted Christ, is hidden away and ministered to by the 144,000. I am confident that anyone who accepts the ministry of the 144,000 will also have divine protection against the terrible things that are happening. The Word shows us that our God of mercy knows how to protect and deliver His own.

During this five-month period, there will be no death.

In those days men will seek death and will not find it (v. 6).

Since death became a reality through the fall of Adam, this is the only occasion in all of God's Word that it takes a holiday.

Men will suffer the torment of the scorpion-like sting of the locusts for five months. The great suffering will cause men to attempt suicide. Whatever they do that would normally result in death will only add to their torment until the five-month period closes.

This is the result of people's determination to live their own way in spite of warnings from God. They have ignored God's love by rejecting Jesus and turning their ears away from the wooing of the Holy Spirit until finally God has no choice but to allow them to go their own way. As the Scripture says, **Therefore they shall eat the fruit of their own way, and be filled to the full with their own fancies** (Prov. 1:31). These horrible things happen not as a result of the will of God for anyone, but as a result of sin and rebellion against God.

The shape of the locusts was like horses prepared for battle. On their heads were crowns of something

like gold, and their faces were like the faces of men. They had hair like women's hair, and their teeth were like lions' teeth.

And they had breastplates like breastplates of iron, and the sound of their wings was like the sound of chariots with many horses running into battle.

They had tails like scorpions, and there were stings in their tails. Their power was to hurt men five months.

And they had as king over them the angel of the bottomless pit, whose name in Hebrew is Abaddon, but in Greek he has the name Apollyon. One woe is past. Behold, still two more woes are coming after these things (vv. 7-12).

The smoke from the bottomless pit causes severe air pollution. People not under the care of the 144,000 are temporarily blinded by the smoke and struggle to breathe. They are helpless to defend themselves against the sting of the locusts.

Some people state, "We believe these locusts represent jet aircraft which have horrible firepower." Have you ever seen an airplane eating grass and leaves off the trees? John's description of the locusts as insects corresponds with an ancient reference found under "locusts" in most encyclopedias. These locusts are literal insects commanded to attack the men who do not have the seal of God on their foreheads.

We should not try to spiritualize everything. Use this law for interpreting God's Word: Interpret literally unless there is a clear figure of speech used within the context of the Scripture. Only then can you use figurative interpretation.

The name of the king over the locusts in both the Hebrew and Greek means "destruction" and "destroyer." One "woe" is past and two more are to come.

The Awesome Army

As the sixth trumpet sounds, four angels bound at the river Euphrates are released:

> Then the sixth angel sounded: And I heard a voice from the four horns of the golden altar which is before God, saying to the sixth angel who had the trumpet, "Release the four angels who are bound at the great river Euphrates" (vv. 13,14).

The angels who rebelled with Satan against God were exiled to earth and bound in chains of darkness. (Jude 6.) These four angels of verse 14 are part of that company of fallen angels.

> So the four angels, who had been prepared for the hour and day and month and year, were released to kill a third of mankind (v. 15).

These four angels are given a fixed period of one year, one month, one day and one hour in which to operate. During that time, they create a vehicle through which they will destroy one-third of the earth's remaining population. That vehicle is an awesome army of 200 million men equipped with weapons of tremendous firepower.

> Now the number of the army of the horsemen was two hundred million; I heard the number of them. And thus I saw the horses in the vision: those who sat on them had breastplates of fiery red, hyacinth blue, and sulfur yellow; and the heads of the horses were like the heads of lions; and out of their mouths came fire, smoke, and brimstone.
>
> By these three plagues a third of mankind was killed — by the fire and the smoke and the brimstone which came out of their mouths. For their power is in their mouth and in their tails; for their tails are like serpents, having heads; and with them they do harm (vv. 16-19).

These are not natural horses which John describes. They have heads like lions out of which come massive destruction. John is describing a military vehicle with awesome firepower which has taken the place of the horse, the most outstanding mode for army transportation in his day. The horse has long since been replaced by powerful, swift, armored vehicles.

The Origin of the Army

Revelation 16 also relates the story of earth. In comparing the verses which describe the sounding of the sixth trumpet in Revelation 9 and the pouring out of the sixth bowl (**vial** KJV) here in Revelation 16:12, we see that both events involve the great river Euphrates:

> **Then the sixth angel poured out his bowl on the great river Euphrates, and its water was dried up, so that the way of the kings from the east might be prepared.**
>
> **Revelation 16:12**

The kings of the East are from the Orient. Matthew 2:1-12 refers to the **wise men from the East** who followed a star to find and worship the Christ child. King Herod asked the wise men when it was that they first saw the star. From this information, Herod knew to order the death of all the children in Bethlehem two years old and under. (v. 16.) Considering the length of time, the distance eastward from Bethlehem places the wise men in the Far East — the Orient.[1]

Only the Orient can produce a 200 million-man army. In December of 1971 the late Chou En-lai, formerly premier and foreign minister of China, declared that China had the potential of fielding a 200 million-man army — the figure specified in Revelation 9!

---

[1] I believe that God created the star for the express purpose of enabling the people from the Orient to find and worship the King of the Jews. The wise men and their attendants were the only ones who saw the star. It is human nature to be curious. If the entire world had seen the star, the following would have been huge. Surely Herod would have learned of the star had it been visible to others.

When the Japanese-Chinese war (begun in the 1930s) officially ended in 1973, the way was paved for diplomatic relationship to be restored between Japan and China. An Oriental federation of nations could easily field an army of 200 million.

The combination of the enormous Chinese population with the industrial ability of the Japanese could create a formidable military machine. The time frame of one year, one month, one day and one hour begins with the twelfth month of the Tribulation's sixth year.[2] In twelve of the thirteen months designated, the 200 million-man army sweeps through Asia to the river Euphrates destroying everything in its path with tremendous firepower. Meeting with some resistance in the world's most-populated areas of Asia, the army destroys one-third of the earth's population.

Russia and China are enemies. Having two fronts, Russia is afraid of China.[3] The Pakistani-Indian war of the last two weeks of December, 1971, was actually a bid for power in Asia between Russia and China. Although Russia lost the war, she won the round.

Diplomatically striving to reach goals they had been unable to achieve militarily, the Chinese had hung up their swords. If they had taken them back down, they would have ruined their initial diplomatic maneuvering.

---

[2]According to Revelation 16:12 the armies of the kings of the East are destroyed at Armageddon. Therefore, we can determine that they left the Far East thirteen months before. After traveling overland for one year, they cross the Euphrates into Israel during the last month of the Tribulation. (This same distance took the kings of Matt. 2 approximately two years, traveling by beast of burden, to follow the special star on their way to worship Him Who was born King of the Jews. The vast modern army will, along the way, meet and destroy opposition, and still arrive at the site of Armageddon in one year.) On the last day they, along with the armies of the Antichrist, are destroyed in one hour.

[3]China will never be militarily involved with Russia (and is no threat to the U.S.). There are no prophetic statements showing China and Russia at war, and China is presently unprepared for global warfare.

Having recently been admitted to the United Nations, the Chinese were anxious to prove themselves. They had to lose the round even though the Pakistanis were horribly crushed by the Russian-backed Indian nation. The Chinese have not forgotten their slap in the face over the event.

When Russia is defeated by Israel, China is pleased. But in her westward attack, she punishes India in Russia's stead. Pray not only for the Chinese and other Orientals who will suffer great losses during the Tribulation, but also for the Indians. Ask God to send a great spiritual revival to India so that many will be swept into His kingdom and escape this terrible destruction. We must do everything God tells us to reach the billions who must be brought into His kingdom. Only Jesus can provide them with an escape from future-prophesied events.

Early in the last month of the seventh year of the Tribulation, the Oriental army arrives at the then-dry river Euphrates. The army crosses and turns south into the nation of Israel. In that final month, its members gather into the Valley of Megiddo which stretches into the plains of the Valley of Jezreel, the site for the Battle of Armageddon.

The European and Mediterranean armies, under the leadership of the Antichrist and the False Prophet, also gather for the Battle of Armageddon.

The Oriental army is under the command of fallen angels, not of the Antichrist. The Orientals are on a collision course with the Antichrist, both forces attempting world conquest. When they discover a common foe — Jesus Christ — they combine forces to resist His return. Of course, their defeat is inevitable. On the final day of the Tribulation, the Orientals and the armies of the Antichrist are destroyed in one hour. This accounts for the last month, one day and one hour.

The Four Categories of Lawlessness

The last verses of Revelation 9 list the major categories of lawlessness occurring during the Tribulation:

> But the rest of mankind, who were not killed by these plagues, did not repent of the works of their hands, that they should not worship demons, and idols of gold, silver, brass, stone, and wood, which can neither see nor hear nor walk.

> And they did not repent of their *murders* or their *sorceries* or their *sexual immorality* or their *thefts* (vv. 20,21).

1. Murder. There will be no regard for life.

2. Sorcery. Witchcraft — sorcery in its most sophisticated and devastating form — coupled with drug use will be the religion. People will follow astrology and attend seances. They will demand the services of spiritual mediums to communicate with the dead, clairvoyants and magicians. These things are abominations to God and are forbidden in His Word.[4]

Any occult activity is pseudoscience, a deceptive operation of Satan to camouflage the extremely destructive practice of witchcraft.

3. Sexual immorality (fornication KJV). There will be no regard for one's morals (if any people remain who have morals) or for one's private person.

4. Theft. No one's private property will be respected. Today lawlessness and preoccupation with the occult are already prevalent. During the Tribulation it will be incredibly worse. Pray for your family, neighbors and the people with whom you work. Pray for your country and its leaders, whether or not you agree with their views.

---

[4]See Leviticus 19 and 20; Deuteronomy 18; Isaiah 47:12-14.

PART IV
The Prophecy
Revelation 10-13, 17, 14, 15
Informational Chapters

11

Revelation 10 and 11
Informational

Because the informational chapters include descriptions of past events, the details of the stories of heaven and earth contained in them are not always chronologically arranged. Keep this in mind as we study the following informational chapters 10-15 and 17.

Revelation 10

The Fourth Unknown

A collection of miscellaneous information, Revelation 10 opens with a reference to seven thunders:

> I saw still another mighty angel coming down from heaven, clothed with a cloud. And a rainbow was on his head, his face was like the sun, and his feet like pillars of fire.
>
> He had a little book open in his hand. And he set his right foot on the sea and his left foot on the land, and cried with a loud voice, as when a lion roars. When he cried out, seven thunders uttered their voices.
>
> Now when the seven thunders uttered their voices, I was about to write; but I heard a voice from heaven saying to me, "Seal up the things which the seven thunders uttered, and do not write them."
>
> Revelation 10:1-4

We don't know what the voices of the seven thunders said. When John was about to reveal this, a voice from heaven stopped him.

We don't know what happened after they spoke. Several references to God "thundering" appear in the Old Testament. For example: **...the Lord thundered with a loud thunder upon the Philistines that day, and so confused them...** (1 Sam. 7:10). God's thundering threw His adversaries into such chaos that they often destroyed themselves.

We cannot speculate as to whether these references provide any insight into the effects of the voices of Revelation 10. *The meaning of the seven thunders is the fourth unknown of Revelation.*

The Time of the Tribulation's End

When the Tribulation has run its course, it will end. Revelation 10 continues:

> **The angel whom I saw standing on the sea and on the land raised up his hand to heaven and swore by Him who lives forever and ever, who created heaven and the things that are in it, the earth and the things that are in it, and the sea and the things that are in it, that there should be delay (time KJV) no longer,**
>
> **but in the days of the sounding of the seventh angel, when he is about to sound, the mystery of God would be finished, as He declared to His servants the prophets** (vv. 5-7).

The mighty angel says, **...that there should be time no longer** (KJV). He is not announcing that time will end, but that *the seven years of Tribulation* will end. When the seventh angel sounds his trumpet (Rev. 11:15), the last day of the Tribulation Period begins. It is then that **the mystery of God would be finished.**

The Tribulation will not be drawn out. For some people that's good news.

Consuming the Word

We know that Jesus and the Word are one: **In the beginning [before all time] was the Word (Christ), and the**

Word was with God, and the Word was God Himself (John 1:1 AMP).

Jesus often spoke of the Word's importance, even calling Himself (the Word) the Bread of Life. The Early Church held the belief that the Word was to be spiritually consumed by and absorbed into the spiritual, or inner, man.

Revelation 10 continues the parallel of the Word as sustenance:

> Then the voice which I heard from heaven spoke to me again and said, "Go, take the little book which is open in the hand of the angel who stands on the sea and on the earth."
>
> So I went to the angel and said to him, "Give me the little book." And he said to me, "Take and eat it; and it will make your stomach bitter, but it will be as sweet as honey in your mouth."
>
> Then I took the little book out of the angel's hand and ate it, and it was as sweet as honey in my mouth. But when I had eaten it, my stomach became bitter (vv. 8-10).

As far as can be determined, **the little book** is the Word of God. Following the angel's instructions, John eats it. In his mouth it was as sweet as honey, but in his belly — his innermost being — it was bitter.

When you first encounter the Word after coming to Jesus, you find simple beauty, wonder and sweetness about it. In those elementary days, you can hardly wait to tell everybody about it.

After a while, you necessarily start growing in the things of God. The Word begins affecting you, bringing you into the likeness of Jesus' mature stature. You have switched diets from the milk to the meat of the Word. The Word is not always as sweet, but is equally as nourishing.

The Fifth Unknown

According to verse 11, John has an assignment to be fulfilled in the future:

> And he said to me, "You must prophesy again about many peoples, nations, tongues, and kings."

When John received the prophecy, he was in his nineties and exiled on the isle of Patmos. We have no record of any other ministry after that time. *When will John have a ministry? As it is future, we will wait and see. This is the fifth unknown of Revelation.*

Revelation 11 — The Two Witnesses

Revelation 11 provides insight into the Two Witnesses' ministry in Jerusalem during the last half of the Tribulation.

Length of the Ministry

> Then I was given a reed like a measuring rod. And the angel stood, saying, "Rise and measure the temple of God, the altar, and those who worship there. But leave out the court which is outside the temple, and do not measure it, for it has been given to the Gentiles. And they will tread the holy city underfoot for forty-two months."
>
> Revelation 11:1,2

The **forty-two months,** exactly three-and-one-half years, covers the last half of the Tribulation Period.[1] The man of sin will have broken his agreement with Israel and established his headquarters in the temple of Jerusalem. (Dan. 9:27; 2 Thess. 2:4.)

---

[1]Because the Two Witnesses' resurrection and catching up occur on the Tribulation's last day (clearly established in Rev. 11), we know that their assignment covers the Tribulation's second half. The sounding of the seventh angelic trumpet (v. 15) sets in motion the events occurring on the Tribulation's final day. Again this identifies the forty-two-month period of verse 2 as being the second half of the Tribulation.

And I will give power to my two witnesses, and they will prophesy one thousand two hundred and sixty days, clothed in sackcloth (v. 3).

One thousand two hundred and sixty days is exactly forty-two months or three-and-one-half years. Time during the Tribulation is based on the prophetic calendar year of 360, not 365, days to the year.[2] This is the reason that the seven years are equally divided into halves of exactly 1,260 days.

Their Identity

Who are the Two Witnesses? Enoch and the apostle John, Elijah or Moses? Joshua and Zerubbabel? None of these? Let's examine the possibilities.

The Two Witnesses have future ministry. Both outstanding prophets, John and Elijah, meet this specification. Of John, Revelation 10:11 states: **And he said to me, "You must prophesy again about many peoples, nations, tongues, and kings."**

The beloved apostle John leaned upon the Lord's breast. (John 13:23.) In addition to the book of Revelation, he wrote the great love letter, The Gospel According to St. John, and three more love epistles. He was the only one of the twelve disciples to die a natural death.

Of Elijah, Malachi 4:5 states: **Behold, I will send you Elijah the prophet before the coming of the great and dreadful day of the Lord.**

When Elijah prayed on Mount Carmel, supernatural fire consumed his sacrifice. (1 Kings 18:22-38.) When he prayed, no rain fell for three-and-one-half years.[3] He appeared on the Mount of Transfiguration with Jesus and Moses, another candidate. (Matt. 17:2,3.) Caught up bodily and alive in a whirlwind, Elijah did not see death. (2 Kings 2:11.)

---

[2] The ancient Jewish calendar allowed for thirty days to the month.
[3] First Kings 17:1; 18:41-45; Luke 4:25.

Before Elijah, Enoch did not see death. A tremendous man of faith, Enoch was also a prophet. He so pleased God that he *was not found* again on the earth because the Lord translated him into His presence. (Gen. 5:24; Heb. 11:5.)

The apostle Paul writes, **It is appointed for men to die once, but after this the judgment** (Heb. 9:27). Because Elijah and Enoch did not see death, they are excellent candidates. However, in the near future, the great number of us who are caught up to meet Jesus in the air will not die. This weakens the possibility of Enoch and Elijah being the witnesses.

Moses was considered the great prophet of Israel and its most outstanding leader. Exodus 7 through 12 record Moses' handling of ten plagues, including one in which he turned water into blood. As we just saw, he appeared upon the Mount of Transfiguration with Jesus. Both John and Moses experienced death, which eliminates them as candidates.

Enoch and Elijah have evidence in their favor, but the ministry of Elijah was fulfilled through John the Baptist. The reincarnationists believe that John was Elijah. John clearly establishes that he was not.

> **And they asked him, "What then? Are you Elijah?" He said, "I am not." "Are you the Prophet?" And he answered, "No."**
>
> **John 1:21**

John the Baptist was sent to fulfill the prophecy in Isaiah 40:3.

> **He said, "I am the voice of one crying in the wilderness: make straight the way of the Lord," as the prophet Isaiah said.**
>
> **John 1:23**

According to Malachi 4:5, Elijah was a forerunner of Christ. Quite evidently, John the Baptist was not Elijah but another forerunner of Christ. As the assignment of Christ is upon us today, the assignment of Elijah was upon John the Baptist.

Revelation 11:4 states:

> **These** (the Two Witnesses) **are the two olive trees and the two lampstands standing before the God of the earth.**

Because the Old Testament refers to Joshua and Zerubbabel as being the olive trees and lampstands that stand before God (see Zech. 4:11-14 AMP), some people have assumed these men are the Two Witnesses. However, the symbolic terminology *olive trees* and *lampstands* is applicable to any believer who on behalf of God's children stands before God. Due to Paul's teaching in Hebrews 9:27, we can eliminate the possibility of Joshua and Zerubbabel being the Two Prophets of Revelation, chapter 11.

You may reason that Elijah has a place of ministry before the appearing or return of Jesus. Other people may think something else. Any opinions held on this matter are pure speculation. *No chapter or verse nails down the Two Witnesses' identities — the sixth unknown of Revelation.*

Personally, I believe that none of the four men we have discussed is either of the Two Witnesses. God is sovereign; He raises up whom He will: **He puts down one, and exalts another** (Ps. 75:7). God chooses 144,000 unmarried men to serve as evangelists during the first four years of the Tribulation. Through their ministry all Israel and many Gentiles are saved. Therefore, God can choose two men out of that same period to be the Two Witnesses.

Don't believe anyone who declares, "The Lord has revealed to me the identity of the Two Witnesses." If someone told me I was one, I'd respond, "No thanks." I'm comfortable with the position that the Lord will raise up the Two Witnesses out of the Tribulation. If I'm mistaken, you can nudge me and say, "Hey, Sutton, you missed it!" I'll answer, "I sure did!" But by then I won't feel bad, because you and I will be standing before God's throne enjoying all the heavenly ceremonies!

Activities

The Two Witnesses have great power. They are divinely immunized from all harm. They command supernatural fire to destroy anyone who attempts to come against them, and they control the plagues and the rain.

> **And if anyone wants to harm them, fire proceeds from their mouth and devours their enemies. And if anyone wants to harm them, he must be killed in this manner.**
>
> **These have power to shut heaven, so that no rain falls in the days of their prophecy; and they have power over waters to turn them to blood, and to strike the earth with all plagues, as often as they desire** (vv. 5,6).

As we have seen, Elijah also prayed and shut off the rain for a three-and-one-half-year period. The drought affected only the land of Israel. As other plagues controlled by the Two Witnesses basically affect only the European-Mediterranean area, it is likely that the same is true of the drought and the plague of rain and hail mixed with blood.

For three-and-one-half years the Two Witnesses carry out their ministry, making life more difficult for the Antichrist. Daily they prophesy the return of the Lord Jesus Christ and number the days until the Antichrist's end in the final battle.

Their Ministry's End

> **When they finish their testimony, the beast that ascends out of the bottomless pit will make war against them, overcome them, and kill them** (v. 7).

The Antichrist repeatedly fails in his attempts to destroy the Two Witnesses until four days before the end of the Tribulation. Their divine protection and use of supernatural fire are withheld, and his forces finally overcome them. Their dead bodies lie on the Jerusalem street for three-and-one-half days in view of the entire world via television. No one is permitted to bury or even touch their bodies.

And their dead bodies will lie in the street of the great city which spiritually is called Sodom and Egypt, where also our Lord was crucified (v. 8).

How could Jerusalem, the Holy City, ever be associated with Sodom and Egypt? The answer lies in our study of both the books of Daniel and Revelation.

Since we know the Antichrist establishes his headquarters in Jerusalem at mid-Tribulation, we begin to have understanding. Daniel 11:37 reveals several things concerning the Antichrist.

One is he has no desire for women; he is a practicing homosexual. That is the reason Jerusalem is known as Sodom in the last three-and-one-half years of the Tribulation. His entrance into Jerusalem draws a crowd of followers like himself.

Furthermore, from Second Thessalonians 2:4, the apostle Paul establishes that the Antichrist announces himself as God, which confirms the last statement of Daniel 11:37. This is tantamount to idolatry for which Egypt has been known since ancient times.

Keep in mind that the False Prophet introduces the worship of the image of the Beast at a mid-Tribulation press conference. This is idolatry in its most flagrant form. The worship of an image is Egyptian in origin.

It is the Antichrist and his followers who bring an evil identity upon the city of Jerusalem where our Lord was crucified.

Then those from the peoples, tribes, tongues, and nations will see their dead bodies three-and-a-half

days, and not allow their dead bodies to be put into graves (v. 9).

The followers of the Antichrist rejoice by having quite a party; but it ends quickly when, slightly before noon on the final day of the Tribulation, the Two Witnesses come back to life!

And those who dwell on the earth will rejoice over them, make merry, and send gifts to one another, because these two prophets tormented those who dwell on the earth. Now after the three-and-a-half days the breath of life from God entered them, and they stood on their feet, and great fear fell on those who saw them (vv. 10,11).

This resurrection alone causes a great emotional upheaval. But then, as the world continues to watch on television, the Two Witnesses are taken up into heaven!

And they heard a loud voice from heaven saying to them, "Come up here." And they ascended to heaven in a cloud, and their enemies saw them (v. 12).

Immediately the most severe upheaval of nature in the earth's history, held in reserve since the opening of the sixth seal (Rev. 6), occurs:

In the same hour there was a great earthquake, and a tenth part of the city fell. In the earthquake seven thousand men were killed, and the rest were afraid and gave glory to the God of heaven.

The second woe is past. Behold, the third woe is coming quickly (vv. 13,14).

The three woes of Revelation 8:13 involve the fifth, sixth and seventh trumpets. After the completion of the second woe, the third woe comes together quickly on the final day of the Tribulation. The seventh and final angelic trumpet sounds producing the Battle of Armageddon and the series of events which end the Tribulation. Let's capsulize the events leading to the seventh angel's trumpet call.

Events Leading to the Tribulation's End

At mid-Tribulation the Antichrist's attempt to assert himself as God triggers God's interference. The Two Witnesses challenge the Antichrist, the angels warn all nations and the plagues begin. The Antichrist's followers want an explanation for his inability to control the circumstances.

During the second half of the Tribulation, the Antichrist is contending with this interference and with rebellious nations, including Egypt.

Four days before Jesus returns to earth, the Antichrist succeeds in killing the Two Witnesses. In the closing hours of the Tribulation as armies gather for the Battle of Armageddon, the Antichrist is well aware that his hour to meet the Lord Jesus is at hand. In view of the world via television, the Two Witnesses, dead for three-and-one-half days, return to life and are raptured. Fear throws the Antichrist's followers into universal pandemonium! Once the witnesses have been caught up, the devastating upheaval of nature erupts.

On the final day of the Tribulation, three major classes of people remain on earth:

1. The followers of the Antichrist.

2. The unsaved people who have not accepted him.

3. The Jewish remnant of Israel.

After the 144,000 are caught up to heaven, only the angels and the Two Witnesses minister. After the death of the witnesses, only the angels proclaim the Gospel. We know they are successful because God's Word does not return void. (Isa. 55:11.) However, many people continue cursing and blaspheming God. As often happens today, incomprehensible as it may seem, the suffering people do not call on God for mercy.

The Third Woe Released

The sounding of the seventh trumpet sets in motion the remaining series of events which end the Tribulation.

> Then the seventh angel sounded: And there were loud voices in heaven, saying, *"The kingdoms of this world have become the kingdoms of our Lord* and of His Christ, and He shall reign forever and ever!"
>
> And the twenty-four elders who sat before God on their thrones fell on their faces and worshiped God, saying: "We give You thanks, O Lord God Almighty, the One who is and who was and who is to come, because You have taken Your great power and reigned.
>
> "The nations were angry, and *Your wrath* (the destruction at the Battle of Armageddon) has come, and the time of the *dead* (the righteous dead of the Tribulation Period), that they should be judged, and that You should reward Your servants the *prophets* (the Two Witnesses), and the *saints* (of the Tribulation Period), and those who fear Your name, small and great, and should destroy *those who destroy the earth"* (the Oriental army and the Antichrist's forces).[4]
>
> Then the temple of God was opened in heaven, and the ark of His covenant was seen in His temple. *And there were lightnings, noises, thunderings, an earthquake, and great hail* (vv. 15-19).

Jesus takes over the world's kingdoms. He returns to earth, then releases a great plague (described in Zechariah 14:12) on the hordes led by the Antichrist. It destroys the merged forces of the 200 million Orientals and the Antichrist's armies at the Battle of Armageddon. The Antichrist and

---

[4] The *dead* are the converts of the 144,000, the Great Multitude of Revelation 7, martyred during the Tribulation. The righteous dead of the Church Age were resurrected when the Church was caught up. The 144,000 are raptured about the end of the fourth year. Both the Great Multitude and the 144,000 are raptured without an accompanying resurrection. The saints to be rewarded at the very end of the Tribulation include the remnant of Israel and those saved through angelic ministry.

False Prophet are cast into the lake of fire and Satan into the bottomless pit, imprisoning him for one thousand years. With this, Jesus fulfills the prophecy of Isaiah 9:6: **...the government will be upon His shoulder.**

The dead are judged. The Tribulation martyrs are avenged and resurrected so that they may take their place in the earthly activities of Jesus' 1,000-year reign and be rewarded. The Two Witnesses are rewarded. The upheaval of nature, described more explicitly in Revelation 6, ends the Tribulation. This terrible day of the Lamb's wrath is unlike any other in history.

Two Different Trumpets

Do not confuse the sounding of the seventh angelic trumpet with the last trumpet of God. In the following two passages, Paul writes of the same trumpet. In the first passage, he calls it **the last trumpet;** in the second, **the trumpet of God.** In both references the trumpet signals the catching up of the Church — the last event of the Church Age.

> **Behold, I tell you a mystery: We shall not all sleep, but we shall all be changed — in a moment, in the twinkling of an eye, at *the last trumpet.* For the trumpet will sound, and the dead will be raised incorruptible, and we shall be changed.**
>
> **1 Corinthians 15:51,52**

> **For the Lord Himself will descend from heaven with a shout, with the voice of an archangel, and with the *trumpet of God.* And the dead in Christ will rise first.**
>
> **Then we who are alive and remain shall be caught up together with them in the clouds to meet the Lord in the air. And thus we shall always be with the Lord.**
>
> **1 Thessalonians 4:16,17**

The scriptural descriptions of the events which follow the sounding of the trumpet of God and the seventh angelic trumpet do not coincide.

The sounding of the trumpet of God described by Paul signals events relating only to the Church. Jesus appears, the dead in Christ are resurrected and the living saints (the Church) are caught up to meet Christ in the air. The Church Age closes.

The sounding of the angelic trumpets of Revelation signals events relating only to the Tribulation Period. We have examined the events following the sounding of the seventh angelic trumpet in the previous pages of this book. With these, the Tribulation closes. Do not allow anyone to convince you that the Church Age and the Tribulation cover the same period.

Additional Proof of Pre-Tribulation Rapture

Notice that following the sound of the seventh trumpet, the Church returns to earth with Christ.[5] If the Church had never gone to heaven, how could it return with Jesus?

The Church participates in the Wedding and the subsequent Marriage Supper of the Lamb. If the Church had not been taken to heaven, how could it participate in those heavenly activities?

Some people explain this by teaching that the Church is not caught up until mid-Tribulation. These people are confusing the Church with the Great Multitude (of Rev. 7) caught up at mid-Tribulation. As we saw, the description of this company is not the same as that of the Church. We also saw that as Jesus is in heaven opening the first seal which begins the Tribulation on earth, the Church is there watching.

The Church being caught up on the final day of the Tribulation would contradict two statements of Jesus. First, of the day of His appearing to receive the glorious Church,

---

[5]Zechariah 14:5; Revelation 17:14; 19:14.

Jesus declared, **But of that day and hour no one knows, not even the angels of heaven, but My Father only** (Matt. 24:36).

Biblically knowledgeable people could count down the last half of the Tribulation's 1,260 days. Should they fail to start their countdown on time, they would be informed of the day of Jesus' return by the Two Witnesses.

Second, Jesus said: **Watch therefore, and pray always that you may be counted worthy to escape all these things that will come to pass, and to stand before the Son of Man** (Luke 21:36).

Things that **will come to pass** happen in the future. If the Church were caught up on the last day of the Tribulation, it would escape the 1,000-year reign of Christ on the earth. This is additional proof that Jesus comes for the Church before the Tribulation.

12

Revelation 12
Informational

This chapter is the prime example of John's adherence to the instructions of writing that which is past, present and future. (Rev. 1:19.) John writes the historical record in order for it to support the story of the future. By inspiration of the Holy Spirit, John ties together past and future events, giving us insight into the entire story of Israel and Jesus Christ in relation to The Revelation.

The first five verses contain three major characters: a dragon, a sun-clothed woman and her male child.

> Now a great sign appeared in heaven: a woman clothed with the sun, with the moon under her feet, and on her head a garland of twelve stars. Then being with child, she cried out in labor and in pain to give birth.
>
> And another sign appeared in heaven: behold, a great, fiery red dragon having seven heads and ten horns, and seven diadems on his heads (vv. 1-3).

Verse 3 contains the first reference in Revelation to the Beast with seven crowned heads and ten horns. We will examine the meaning of these crowned heads in our discussion of Revelation 13.

The Dragon

The identity of the dragon is clear.

> His tail drew a third of the stars of heaven and threw them to the earth. And the dragon stood before

> **the woman who was ready to give birth, to devour her Child as soon as it was born. She bore a male Child who was to rule all nations with a rod of iron. And her Child was caught up to God and His throne (vv. 4,5).**

Without question, the dragon is Satan. His identity becomes completely established by the end of the twelfth chapter. However, there has been much controversy within the Church concerning the identity of the woman and the male child.

The Woman

Revelation 12 gives us insight into the tremendous story of the woman who brings forth the male child. Simply, the woman is Israel; the male child, Jesus.

Some people teach that the woman is the great institutional church; the male child, a special company of overcomers within it who are the Bride of Christ. They teach that only this special Bride company will be caught up to heaven.

If this is true, the institutional church, as the woman, will be provided with a special hiding place until the end of the Tribulation. This leaves no one to form the harlot church of Revelation 17.

If this teaching is true, the people in the institutional church who are not part of the special company of overcomers are the *remnant* of Revelation 12. This remnant is clearly composed of Israelis, not the "leftovers" of the institutional church. Avoid teachings which cannot be harmonized with the whole scriptural record. They prohibit correct interpretation of Revelation.

Some people mistakenly identify the world's institutional religious bodies as *the Church*. The teachings of both Jesus and Paul establish that the Church is the company of born-again, Spirit-led followers of the Lord

Jesus who keep God's Word! (Although the institutional church and the true Church are not in any way the same, the members of the Church may be associated with religious groups and are often found within them.)

A reference from the Old Testament further confirms the sun-clothed woman's identity as Israel. The sun, moon and eleven stars of a dream Joseph told his brothers clearly depict the household of Jacob, or Israel:

> **Then he dreamed still another dream and told it to his brothers, and said, "Look, I have dreamed another dream. And this time, the sun, the moon, and the eleven stars bowed down to me."**
>
> **So he told it to his father and his brothers; and his father rebuked him and said to him, "What is this dream that you have dreamed? Shall your mother and I and your brothers indeed come to bow down to the earth before you?"**
>
> **Genesis 37:9,10**

The Male Child

The male child of Revelation 12:5 can only be Jesus. This verse clearly states that the male child is caught up to God, to His throne, and shall rule all nations with a rod of iron (Rev. 19:15).

The Church will also be caught up to God and will rule with Christ on earth. However, the Church gets its authority through Jesus. Furthermore, verse 4 tells us that Satan is ready to devour the male child the moment the child is born. The Church was not placed in the world to be destroyed by Satan, but to be the instrument God uses to wreck Satan's stronghold.[1]

We see a parallel to verse 4 in Matthew 1 and 2. In this account, Satan is greatly desiring to destroy the Christ child

---

[1]See Matthew 16:18; Ephesians 6:10; First Corinthians 10.

immediately after His birth. This again identifies the male child as Jesus.

Satan Is Not All-Knowing

Joseph had traveled slowly to Bethlehem because of Mary's pregnant condition. By the time they arrived, due to no fault of the innkeeper, no room was left in the inn. They were offered the next best place for warmth and protection from the elements — the stables.

Satan could not locate the Christ child. Even his number-one agent, King Herod, could not acquire the information through his astrologers, soothsayers, clairvoyants or those who dealt in witchcraft. These advisers had to refer to the prophetic Scripture to determine Jesus' birthplace as Bethlehem! Herod shared this information with the kings of the East, hoping they would learn the Christ child's location and, in turn, tell him. But when warned by God of Herod's sinister heart, the Oriental kings left Bethlehem and returned home.

After learning of their departure, Herod issued a decree for the death of all children in the Bethlehem area two years old and under. Following the instructions of an angel who appeared to him, Joseph took Mary and the Christ child to Egypt for their safekeeping. They did not return to the land of Israel until it was safe.

This account points out an outstanding truth: Satan had insufficient information to locate the Christ child! Notice how God outfoxed Satan!

Had Jesus been born in the best accommodations, Satan could have easily located Him. But Satan did not expect a child of majestic importance, destined for kingship, to be born in an inconspicuous, lowly place. From this we see that Satan is not all-knowing and omnipresent as is God. If he were, the Christ child could not have been hidden!

The 144,000

Some people teach that the male child of Revelation 12:5 is the 144,000 selected Jewish men. However, upon their selection the 144,000 are not set upon by Satan to be destroyed. In fact, they have divine immunization and move unhindered in their evangelism.[2] During this first half of the Tribulation, the man destined to be the Antichrist is fully occupied attempting to establish his domain diplomatically, politically and economically. He is in no position to act against the 144,000 Jewish evangelists. Only Jesus fits the identity of the male child with ease.

The woman is Israel, not the institutional church. She brings forth a male child who is caught up to God and who will rule all nations with firm authority. In the most exact biblical sense, the woman is Israel and the male child, Jesus. These simple identities totally harmonize with the entire biblical account.

The next section of Revelation 12 describes Satan's fall.

Satan's Total Defeat

Satan Cast Out of Heaven

> And war broke out in heaven: Michael and his angels fought with the dragon; and the dragon and his angels fought, but they did not prevail... (vv. 7,8).

The dragon was unable to destroy the male child, Jesus Christ, upon His birth!

> ...nor was a place found for them in heaven any longer.
>
> So the great dragon was cast out, that serpent of old, called the Devil and Satan, who deceives the whole world; he was cast to the earth, and his angels were cast out with him (vv. 8,9).

[2]Because the 144,000 are sealed by having the Father's name written in their foreheads, they have divine immunization. (See Rev. 7,14; Ezek. 9.)

When Satan was defeated and cast out of heaven, one-third of the angels fell with him. **His tail drew a third of the stars of heaven and threw them to the earth** (v. 4). (As we saw when studying Rev. 1, the word *star* often identifies angels.)

> **Then I heard a loud voice saying in heaven, "Now salvation, and strength, and the kingdom of our God, and the power of His Christ have come, for the accuser of our brethren, who accused them before our God day and night, has been cast down.**
>
> **"And they overcame him (Satan) by the blood of the Lamb and by the word of their testimony, and they did not love their lives to the death.**
>
> **"Therefore rejoice, O heavens, and you who dwell in them! Woe to the inhabitants of the earth and the sea! For the devil has come down to you, having great wrath, because he knows that he has a short time"** (vv. 10-12).

Some believe that Satan and his angels come and go in heaven as they please, literally approaching God's throne and accusing the saints.

If this is true, the war between Michael and his angels and the devil and his angels has not occurred, and Satan has not been cast out of heaven. This means Satan's initial rebellion against God, when he hoped to usurp God's authority and replace Him, continues to this day. God's Word makes this story difficult to accept. Jesus Himself declared that He saw Satan fall from heaven. (Luke 10:18.) Revelation 12:10 tells us that once Satan has been cast down, several events follow: salvation and spiritual life through Jesus Christ, and the beginning of God's kingdom on earth. (v. 10.)

If Satan still has personal access to God's throne to accuse the brethren, salvation has not come, God's kingdom on earth has not begun and Christ's power has not manifested on earth. Therefore, we cannot overcome Satan through the blood of the Lamb or by the word of our testimonies. If true, these last five points directly contradict what the Scriptures teach is available!

God has declared that the devil is a liar, and there is no truth in him. (John 8:44.) Our heavenly Father wouldn't believe Satan's story over one of His children's! The entirety of the Word reveals that God is all-knowing. When one of His children commits a disobedient act or allows temptation to draw him into sin, He knows immediately. He doesn't have to wait to get His information from the devil!

God has sent the Holy Spirit, not Satan, to help man recognize his disobedient acts and restore him to fellowship. Anyone who overrides the Holy Spirit's operation leaves himself open for a vicious satanic attack.

Even though Satan is the accuser of the brethren, he cannot accuse them before God. The only brethren Satan has ever been able to accuse before God's throne were his fellow angels before his fall.

Satan accuses the brethren before others and themselves. He works overtime, continually inspiring Christians to find fault with each other. This prevents them from having fellowship or from working together, delaying the full formation of the Body of Christ. (See 1 Cor. 12.)

If Satan is unsuccessful in accusing one Christian to another, he will accuse one to himself. If you allow this to happen, he will back you into a corner, hand you his club of self-condemnation and leave you beating yourself. This frees him to find somebody else he can accuse.

Today many Christians are living under condemnation, a work of the devil. The Holy Spirit doesn't bring condemnation but conviction, a work of love.

Ephesians 2:2 supplies further proof that Satan has been cast out of heaven. It refers to him as the prince of the power of the air. This shows us Satan has access to the immediate heavens surrounding the earth, but not to the abode of God. Our space program has provided physical evidence attesting to this.

Space missions have probed the stratosphere into the very front yard of God. Until recently, all returning astronauts underwent extensive quarantine and thorough examination for disease and contamination. Now astronauts are no longer quarantined upon their return from space, because scientists have discovered that no bacteria or harmful elements of any kind exist beyond the atmosphere of the earth.

The Bible clearly reveals that Satan is the originator of sickness, disease and all evil. If he were still in the heavens, his pollution could be found there as it is on earth.

Incidentally, upon returning from space, our astronauts often declare that they have seen the glories of God. "We are more convinced than ever before of the existence of God," some have said, "for His handiwork is so evident." Not one has reported sensing any evil influence in space.

Our examination of the dragon, the sun-clothed woman and the story of angelic warfare has made us more knowledgeable about our adversary, the devil. Revelation 12 clearly shows that Satan and his angels have absolutely no access to heaven. It reaches into the authority of preexisting Scriptures to give account of Satan's fall.[3]

After this fall, Satan was able to upset many of God's earthly plans. Finally God administered Satan's ultimate defeat by sending Jesus Christ to provide salvation.

---

[3]See Isaiah 14; Ezekiel 28; and the book of Genesis.

Remember, Satan is not omnipresent or all-knowing; he is only a liar and an accuser. God's Word gives us the authority and effective tools of the blood of the Lamb and the word of our testimony to use against him. If you have used these, you have experienced their effectiveness. Men and women abiding in God through Jesus are more than conquerors and more than a match for Satan!

No one need be devil-conscious. Just know how to recognize and deal with the adversary when he shows up. Continue being victorious in the name of the Lord.

The Weakness of the Flesh Overcome

God chose a people, Israel, through whom He could work to bless the whole earth. Satan worked against those people.

Verse 13 states:

Now when the dragon (Satan) saw that he had been cast to the earth, he persecuted the woman who gave birth to the male Child.

History records that after Israel produced the male child, her situation progressively worsened. If it were possible for Satan to succeed in his repeated attempts to destroy the entire Israeli race, much of God's Word could never be fulfilled, making it void. Satan could then accuse God of being incapable of keeping His Word. For this reason, God has directly intervened every time Satan has attempted to destroy the Jewish race.

Satan hindered God's initial plans in the Garden of Eden. When God brought forth the Law to counter this spiritual setback, Satan began work to make the Law ineffective. The Law was perfect. But because of the weakness of human flesh, Satan was again able to upset God's plan. When God sent Jesus to completely remedy the situation (as prophesied in Gen. 3:15), Satan was incapable of hindering God's plan, because he could not overcome Jesus. Paul wrote:

> **For the law of the Spirit of life in Christ Jesus has made me free from the law of sin and death.**
>
> **For what the law could not do in that it was weak through the flesh, God did by sending His own Son in the likeness of sinful flesh, on account of sin: He condemned sin in the flesh.**
>
> **Romans 8:2,3**

To overcome Satan, Jesus came in the weakness of the flesh. By exercising God-given strength over weaknesses, He defeated Satan on every count. As long as we recognize Jesus as the Source of our strength, we, His followers, can overcome. Remember Paul's words, **...when I am weak, then I am strong** (2 Cor. 12:10).

We have no excuse for allowing Satan to take advantage of us through the weakness of the flesh. Hold fast to the biblical truth that Jesus has already overcome all areas of weakness and provided for us the spiritual ability to be strong. Because He has defeated Satan, we have defeated Satan. This is an exciting discovery! Through Christ we are more than conquerors. Greater is Jesus Who is in us than Satan who is in the world. (Rom. 8:37; 1 John 4:4.)

Satan Always Fails

The first five verses of Revelation 12 cover the time from the birth of Christ into the last half of the Tribulation. In verse 6 we read John's prophecy concerning the remnant of Israel, picked up again in verse 14:

> **Then the woman (Israel) fled into the wilderness, where she has a place prepared by God, that they should feed her there one thousand two hundred and sixty days.**
>
> **But the woman was given two wings of a great eagle, that she might fly into the wilderness to her place, where she is nourished for a time and times and half a time, from the presence of the serpent (vv. 6,14).**

The eagle could easily be identified as the United States, Israel's present sponsor. The only great eagle nation, the United States, is capable of quickly airlifting Israelis to a hiding place.[4]

From verse 6 we know that the length of **a time and times and half a time** (v. 14) equals 1,260 days (forty-two months or three-and-one-half years). During the last half of the Tribulation, the woman, the remnant of Israel (which had not accepted Christ as the Messiah by mid-Tribulation), will be given a special place of hiding (on the earth) from the Antichrist (the serpent) for the preservation of the Jewish race.

When Satan cannot find the remnant of Israelis, his plans are again fouled. He was unable to destroy the Great Multitude and the 144,000 Jewish evangelists. The 144,000 had divine immunization; both groups were caught up to heaven. Every time Satan put his vehicle in motion, God interfered and stopped him.

Some people have taught that after Jesus appears and catches up the Church, God turns earth and its population over to Satan. Satan then comes forth with the Antichrist, the mark of the Beast and false religion to subdue the whole world. The Tribulation is indeed a difficult period. However, Satan has never won a round and will not begin by winning any during the Tribulation. His plans and those of his agent, the Antichrist, continually fail.

Because his program doesn't work, the Antichrist becomes the most frustrated human on earth.

So the serpent spewed water out of his mouth like a flood after the woman, that he might cause her to be carried away by the flood (v. 15).

---

[4]The exact location of the wilderness and origin of the eagle's wings is another of the unknowns of Revelation.

From other uses of the word *flood* in the Scriptures, we know that the **flood** of verse 15 is not of water but of words coming from Satan through the man he has chosen to be the Antichrist. The Antichrist, a tremendous orator (see Dan. 7:8,11,25; 8), attempts to convince the people among whom the remnant has been hidden to destroy the Israelis. Here is what happens:

> **But the earth helped the woman, and the earth opened its mouth and swallowed up the flood which the dragon had spewed out of his mouth (v. 16).**

Literally interpreted, this verse means that whatever the Antichrist does in his attempt to destroy the remnant of Israel is swallowed up by an act of nature, as were Korah and his company. (Num. 16:29-35.) Since the remnant is hidden until the indignation is past (Rev. 12:14; Isa. 26:20,21), they cannot be pursued by armies. The earth swallowing up the flood means the Antichrist's words are rejected by the people among whom the remnant is hidden.

> **And the dragon was enraged with the woman, and he went to make war with the rest of her offspring, who keep the commandments of God and have the testimony of Jesus Christ (v. 17).**

The description of the forces of the Antichrist waging war in an attempt to destroy the remnant of Israel places this event as occurring shortly after mid-Tribulation. The remnant has **the testimony of Jesus Christ**, indicating they have accepted Jesus as their Messiah. We know that they, as members of the elect,[5] survive this attack. When Jesus returns, He calls His elect to Himself from all over the earth.

> **And He will send His angels with a great sound of a trumpet, and they will gather together His elect from the four winds, from one end of heaven to the other.**
> **Matthew 24:31**

---

[5]There are four elects: Israel (Isa. 43:4), the Church (Col. 3:11,12), angels (1 Tim. 5:31) and Jesus (1 Pet. 2:6).

With the reference to the remnant's salvation, an event which precedes Jesus' return, Revelation 12 has informed us of Israel's history from the birth of Christ through the Church Age and most of the Tribulation.

13
Revelation 13
The Beast System
Informational

Revelation 13 provides detailed insight into the meaning of the Beast with seven crowned heads and ten horns, the dragon introduced by Revelation 12:3. The Beast is a system created by Satan. With Satan as its direct source of power and basis for authority, it is like him.

The System

In the following vivid description of the Beast, John uses the name **blasphemy**, which further identifies this Beast with Satan:

> **Then I stood on the sand of the sea. And I saw a beast rising up out of the sea, having seven heads and ten horns, and on his horns ten crowns, and on his heads a blasphemous name (v. 1).**

The Beast is the product of Satan's work through people. The sea out of which it comes is not a body of water but masses of people — the sea of humanity. Just as God accomplishes His plan through human agents, Satan can only use the same vehicle.

The dragon of Revelation 12 has seven crowned heads. Each represents a kingdom or great empire. According to Revelation 13, the ten horns are also crowned, indicating that each exists as a nation ruled by a leader.

> Now the beast which I saw was like a leopard, his
> feet were like the feet of a bear, and his mouth like the
> mouth of a lion. The dragon gave him his power, his
> throne, and great authority (v. 2).

The symbolism of the animals identifies this Beast with
the prophecies of Daniel:

> Daniel spoke, saying, "I saw in my vision by night,
> and behold, the four winds of heaven were stirring up
> the Great Sea. And four great beasts came up from the
> sea, each different from the other.
>
> "The first was like a lion, and had eagle's wings. I
> watched till its wings were plucked off; and it was
> lifted up from the earth and made to stand on two feet
> like a man, and a man's heart was given to it.
>
> "And suddenly another beast, a second, like a bear.
> It was raised up on one side, and had three ribs in its
> mouth between its teeth. And they said thus to it:
> 'Arise, devour much flesh!'
>
> "After this I looked, and there was another, like a
> leopard, which had on its back four wings of a bird.
> The beast also had four heads, and dominion was given
> to it.
>
> "After this I saw in the night visions, and behold, a
> fourth beast, dreadful and terrible, exceedingly strong.
> It had huge iron teeth; it was devouring, breaking in
> pieces, and trampling the residue with its feet. It was
> different from all the beasts that were before it, and it
> had ten horns.
>
> "I was considering the horns, and there was another
> horn, a little one, coming up among them, before whom
> three of the first horns were plucked out by the roots.
> And there, in this horn, were eyes like the eyes of a
> man, and a mouth speaking pompous words."[1]
>
> **Daniel 7:2-8**

---

[1] The little horn of verse 8 refers to the Antichrist. The description of the man who
will become the Antichrist correlates perfectly with John's description.

Daniel was the only prophet who had all-inclusive insight into the times of the Gentiles as related to Israel's captivity. The Gentile Age began with the captivity of Israel (721-608 B.C.) and will reach its conclusion with Israel's restoration (1948 A.D. until the Millennium). From its beginning, the times of the Gentiles produce the great empires: Babylonian, Medo-Persian, Greek and Roman. Later in this study we will examine two empires which existed before these four.

Daniel interpreted a dream for King Nebuchadnezzar. (See Dan. 2.) In the dream was a great image with a head of gold, chest and arms of silver, belly (**loins** KJV) and thighs of bronze (**brass** KJV), legs of iron, and feet and toes of iron and clay.

The golden head represented the Babylonian Empire; the silver breast, the Medo-Persian Empire; the brass loins and thighs, the empire of Greece under Alexander the Great; and the legs, feet and toes of iron and clay, the great Roman Empire. The Roman Empire had two major divisions, symbolized by the legs and feet; and ten subdivisions, symbolized by the ten toes, which correspond to the ten horns.

The Beast with seven crowned heads and ten crowned horns symbolizes the same system as Nebuchadnezzar's dream and Daniel's vision. (Dan. 2 and 7.) Keep in mind that this entire satanic system of governments, commerce and religion is called the Beast.

The Seal Lifted

People in the past were unable to understand the prophetic Scriptures as clearly as we can today. The following verse gives us the reason:

> **But you, Daniel, shut up the words, and seal the book until the time of the end; many shall run to and fro, and knowledge shall increase.**
>
> **Daniel 12:4**

A seal, placed on prophecies pertaining to the Gentile Age in relation to Israel's captivity and restoration, prevented those prophecies from coming to pass until the time of the end (when the Church Age ends so that the next age may begin).

According to the above verse we know that the time of the end has arrived when an explosion of knowledge and a great mobility of man occurs. These two outstanding things will primarily affect the believing Church company, the ones upon whom God is depending, not the so-called "spiritually enlightened" who never settle nor accept responsibility anywhere.

Daniel 12 establishes clearly that, when the seal is lifted, the righteous begin a great quest for the knowledge of God, flowing with other believers to receive teaching.

The world has become much more mobile and knowledgeable since World War II. Undoubtedly, God has raised up the most outstanding teachers and ministers for this final generation of the Church Age. No longer limited to a specific location, believers can travel to hear these anointed men of God. This widespread traveling also serves to acquaint the believers with one another.

Since the world's knowledge is definitely increasing in this space age, a corresponding increase of knowledge on the spiritual level should also be evident among the saints. Increased knowledge of the Word will change some of our traditional teachings, bringing perfection. Because of the knowledge explosion and increased mobility since World War II, we can declare that the seal has been lifted. At that time, prophecy also began being fulfilled at a rapid pace.

As long as the seal was intact, the Holy Spirit did not violate it in order to reveal the prophetic Scriptures' full content prematurely. Now that the seal is gone and prophecy is being fulfilled, we have a distinct advantage over Bible scholars of the past. We need no longer speculate. Past inaccuracies of prophetic interpretation are exposed.

For years prophetic teachers, knowing little about the Beast System and its operation, taught only about the Antichrist. Since the Holy Spirit has opened the prophetic Scriptures to our understanding, we have discovered that the Beast is more than a man. The Beast refers to an entire system and two men.

The Beast's Fatal Wound

I saw one of his heads as if it had been mortally wounded, and his deadly wound was healed. And all the world marveled and followed the beast.
Revelation 13:3

Some teachers declare that the man who heads the Beast System, the Antichrist, will be assassinated, then resurrected by the False Prophet to deceive the whole world. Such teaching is unsound and unharmonious with the entire biblical story. It would be impossible for the False Prophet to resurrect the Antichrist, because only God the Holy Ghost has resurrection power, and He would not resurrect this ungodly man.

One of the Beast's heads is wounded unto death. Each head represents a kingdom. Because the seal of Daniel 12 has been lifted, we know from studying the biblical and historical records that the Beast's fatal wound is the destruction of one of the great empires, the Roman Empire.

In Nebuchadnezzar's dream a stone destroys the great image. The stone represents the first coming of Jesus. The Church Age begins, wounding the sixth head to death.

The fall of the Roman Empire causes the demise of the entire system, which will indeed be resurrected by Satan, amazing all the world.

Preceding his statement concerning the wounded head (v. 3), John is still supplying information about the total system he calls the Beast. The man who eventually heads the system is also called a beast. Remember to differentiate between the two. It is the system and not the man who is mortally wounded.

So far, we have examined only the Beast System and not the man who heads it. With verse 5 John begins referring to the man who will have authority and head the vast system.

The Antichrist

So they worshiped the dragon who gave authority to the beast; and they worshiped the beast, saying, "Who is like to the beast? Who is able to make war with him?"

And he was given a mouth speaking great things and blasphemies, and he was given authority to continue for forty-two months (vv. 4,5).

The Beast System will be given a voice which speaks **great things and blasphemies.** He will be **given authority to continue for forty-two months.** As is generally known, the man who will become the Antichrist does not take this image upon himself until the last half of the Tribulation. During the first half he attempts to pass himself off as a man of peace.

He will be an outstanding leader of the European states, a diplomat of the first order. Using his ability to combine the governments, commerce, military and religion of the ten nations, he affects the resurrection of the Beast System.

He is so successful in establishing his system that the nations with which he is associated make him their head. We have seen that at mid-Tribulation he begins his attempt to conquer the world. Breaking his agreement with Israel, he begins pursuing the office of world president or dictator.

However, Jesus is the only man who will ever succeed in ruling this world.

> **Then he opened his mouth in blasphemy against God, to blaspheme His name, His tabernacle, and those who dwell in heaven (v. 6).**

The Antichrist blasphemes the many people who have escaped him and his system, but to no avail. They are in heaven!

> **It was granted to him to make war with the saints and to overcome them. And authority was given him over every tribe, tongue, and nation (v. 7).**

The Church company is already before the throne of God as this scene takes place. The saints referred to in the above verse are not the believers of the Church Age but the saints of the Tribulation, the converts of the 144,000 Jewish evangelists.

Verse 7 states that the Antichrist was given power over all kindreds, languages and nations. Verse 2 reveals that Satan gave him that authority. He has satanic authority and power to make war against and overcome the 144,000, their converts and the hidden remnant of Israel, but finds this impossible. Remember, Satan has used numerous other men through the centuries in his attempt to crush the Church and gain control over the world.

Satan's power and authority do not begin to compare with God's. If the Antichrist's assignment were from God, he would succeed. However, since it is from Satan, he fails despite the tremendous vehicles he has with which to work. After the Antichrist breaks his agreement with Israel at mid-Tribulation, he attempts to make war with her people. He fails because the converts of the 144,000 are caught up to heaven and the remnant of Israel is hidden away.

The statements in verse 7 are much less awesome when tied to the information in verse 2. The idea of the Antichrist and his system having absolute authority is properly diminished to fit the rest of the story.

> **All who dwell on the earth will worship him** (the Antichrist), **whose names have not been written in the Book of Life of the Lamb slain from the foundation of the world.**
>
> **If anyone has an ear, let him hear.**
>
> **He who leads into captivity shall go into captivity; he who kills with the sword must be killed with the sword. Here is the patience and the faith of the saints** (vv. 8-10).

Please do not take the phrase, **all who dwell on the earth**, as literal and all-inclusive. Doing so would include the 144,000 Jewish evangelists, the remnant of Israel, the Arabs who resist the Antichrist (Zech. 14; Isa. 19) and many Gentiles (Zech. 8:23) as worshiping the Antichrist.

The statement, **If anyone has an ear, let him hear,** clearly reveals that God is attempting to gain the attention of all people during this time. God is saying, "If you listen to and obey Me, you won't be caught in this satanic system."

He further emphasizes that destruction awaits those people who foolishly become part of the Antichrist system. Therefore, He calls on the saints, or saved ones, of that period to remain patient and continue in the faith.

The False Prophet

John finds the descriptive word *beast* useful in referring to the entire system and the two men who lead it.

Verse 11 discloses the third character John identifies as a beast, known as the False Prophet:

> **Then I saw another beast coming up out of the earth, and he had two horns like a lamb and spoke like a dragon.**

Deceptively, the False Prophet has a religious identity: he looks like a lamb, but speaks like a dragon.

And he exercises all the authority of the first beast in his presence, and causes the earth and those who dwell in it to worship the first beast, whose deadly wound was healed.

He performs great signs, so that he even makes fire come down from heaven on the earth in the sight of men.

And he deceives those who dwell on the earth by those signs which he was granted to do in the sight of the beast, telling those who dwell on the earth to make an image to the beast who was wounded by a sword and lived.

He was granted power to give breath to the image of the beast, that the image of the beast should both speak and cause as many as would not worship the image of the beast to be killed (vv. 12-15).

The False Prophet immediately brings great deception, causing many people on the earth to worship the Beast System. He has cunning occult powers.

Of the Antichrist's operation, Paul says there will be **lying wonders** (2 Thess. 2:9). These are clever maneuvers designed to appear as genuine miracles in an attempt to deceive all mankind. None of the acts of either the Antichrist or the False Prophet are true miracles.

The False Prophet has an image created of the Beast and threatens with death all who do not worship it. Keep in mind that the Beast System is not worldwide but operating from its European base. Worship of the image introduces idolatry, which God has always rejected. (Lev. 26:1.)

The Mark of the Beast

He causes all, both small and great, rich and poor, free and slave, to receive a mark on their right hand or on their foreheads, and that no one may buy or sell except one who has the mark or the name of the beast, or the number of his name. Here is wisdom. Let him

who has understanding calculate the number of the
beast, for it is the number of a man: His number is 666
(vv. 16-18).

According to biblical numerology, a man's number is
six. The number *six* indicates "incompleteness." The
number of the Beast System is three sixes. Therefore, this
system is an incomplete operation which will fail. Since
the entire structure has been designed by the dragon
(Satan), it is very destructive but imperfect. Again we
visualize the evil trinity: Satan, the Antichrist and the
False Prophet.

As the Tribulation progresses, the situation on earth
becomes increasingly more critical, especially during the
last half. Particularly in the geographical areas held by the
Beast System, there will be less commercial operation,
because there will be very little left to buy or sell due to
famine and wars. However, through the mark of the Beast,
the Antichrist attempts to take over as much of the world's
remaining commercial operation as possible.

To continue buying and selling, one must take the mark
of the system's identification on either the right hand or the
forehead. The system uses the mark and the threat of death
to coerce people into surrender. Of course, they that take
the mark or worship the Beast's image seal their doom.
There is no possibility of salvation for them. (Rev. 14:9-11.)

There has been great controversy and speculation over
the exact design of the mark. Its most outstanding
characteristic will be its association with the number 666.
We should not speculate about its design beyond this,
because the Scripture is not specific.

Some people become upset when a phone number,
street address or license plate contains the number 666.
Someone has pointed out that the license number on many
of the commercial vehicles in Israel begins with an ominous

666.[2] This is superstition! The number 666 itself is not significant. However, when it identifies all those people who become part of the Beast System, it will become significant.

Today we live in a time of forerunners. For the sake of speed and efficiency, every major concern identifies its customers by an account number. Our accounting system is not satanic; our use of credit cards and Social Security is not of the Antichrist. These systems are only forerunners of the Antichrist's attempts to take over world commerce.

The Antichrist and the False Prophet have a period of exactly seven years to attempt to carry out their plan for world conquest. At mid-Tribulation, they take over governments. They attempt to take over religion by calling for worship of the Beast, which is idolatry, and commerce, by the issuance of the identification mark. The Antichrist is ready to promote himself. He moves into the Jerusalem temple and exalts himself above all that is called God.

Let no one deceive you by any means; for that Day will not come unless the falling away comes first, and the man of sin is revealed, the son of perdition, who opposes and exalts himself above all that is called God or that is worshiped, so that he sits as God in the temple of God, showing himself that he is God.

2 Thessalonians 2:3,4

The Antichrist promotes himself at the expense of his own system and anyone in his way. He has one major problem: God continually gets in his way!

The Beast System is most successful in the European-Mediterranean area. Since the Arabs reject the system and survive, I am convinced many other nations also survive the Tribulation.[3]

---

[2]Many commercial vehicles owned by Arabs in Israel have license plate numbers beginning with 666. Through this method, the Israelis can quickly identify the Arabs in case of emergency.

[3]Isaiah 19:23-25; Ezekiel 38:13; Zechariah 14:18,19.

14
Revelation 17
The Harlot
Informational

Revelation 17 offers excellent explanation of what Revelation 13 sets forth. Because these two chapters connect so perfectly, we are examining them consecutively for more fruitful understanding.

Her Identity

The harlot is the personification of false religion. She is the amalgamation of all man's religions into one organization.

> Then one of the seven angels who had the seven bowls came and talked with me, saying to me, "Come, I will show you the judgment of the great harlot who sits on many waters, with whom the kings of the earth committed fornication, and the inhabitants of the earth were made drunk with the wine of her fornication."
>
> So he carried me away in the Spirit into the wilderness. And I saw a woman sitting on a scarlet beast which was full of names of blasphemy, having seven heads and ten horns (vv. 1-3).

The **waters** of verse 1 are peoples, nations, races and languages. (v. 15.) This **great harlot (whore** KJV) has had such vast influence over masses of people that she has been able to control entire nations. The kings of the earth have committed fornication with her, and the inhabitants of the earth are drunk with the wine of her fornication. What a horrible scene!

Fornication refers to false religion, which has a form of godliness but denies the power thereof. (2 Tim. 3:5 KJV.) It substitutes religious rights and membership for true repentance and salvation. God considers all people who worship anyone or anything besides Himself participants in spiritual fornication and adultery. He includes even those who are sincere in their involvement. The woman, identified as the harlot, is carrying on an affair with the Beast.

Revelation 17 reveals additional information about the Beast System. The seven heads are great kingdoms; the ten horns, lesser kingdoms. The harlot of Revelation has been supported by the Beast System since its beginning.

> **The woman was arrayed in purple and scarlet, and adorned with gold and precious stones and pearls, having in her hand a golden cup full of abominations and the filthiness of her fornication. And on her forehead a name was written: MYSTERY, BABYLON THE GREAT, THE MOTHER OF HARLOTS AND OF THE ABOMINATIONS OF THE EARTH (vv. 4,5).**

In this description and list of names, MYSTERY is the first name that identifies the harlot. She is of a religious nature — mystical, spiritualistic. Close historical examination reveals that she dominated the seven great empires supporting her. It is not surprising to note that spiritualist mediums or people who practiced witchcraft controlled the leaders of the great empires from the time of Egypt until the fall of the Roman Empire.

The harlot's second title is BABYLON THE GREAT, identifying the harlot religious system with Babylon and every successive Gentile empire. This clearly shows that the harlot began to exert her influence within the Gentile empires.

The harlot's third title, THE MOTHER OF HARLOTS, indicates that every evil and destructive thing on earth results from the operation of Satan through her.

Her fourth title, THE MOTHER OF...ABOMINATIONS OF THE EARTH, reveals her total rejection by God.

Her Length of Operation

I saw the woman, drunk with the blood of the saints and with the blood of the martyrs of Jesus. And when I saw her, I marveled with great amazement (v. 6).

The harlot has operated over a vast period of time. The Gentile empires resulted from Israel's collapse and captivity.

History records that with the Assyrian Empire the system was ushered in. The Egyptian Empire, the first head of the Beast System, enslaved the family of Israel. When God delivered them, they established the great nation of Israel. Then came their rebellion and captivity. Assyria was the Gentile empire which initiated Israel's captivity by taking the ten northern tribes. The southern tribes of Judah were taken into Babylonian captivity about 107 years later. Thus Nebuchadnezzar's dream (Dan. 2) begins with the Babylonian Empire after Israel's total captivity.

With the fall of the Roman Empire, the entire system crumbled. The harlot, which had a controlling influence on Gentile empires, was responsible for the death of many of God's saints, including those of the Early Church. In Revelation 17, as in chapter 12, John is tying historical records to future events.

...And when I saw her, I marveled with great amazement. But the angel said to me, "Why did you marvel? I will tell you the mystery of the woman and of the beast that carries her, which has the seven heads and the ten horns. The beast that you saw was, and is not, and will ascend out of the bottomless pit and go to perdition..." (vv. 6-8).

Again John refers to the entire satanic system. As history records the empires, the Bible confirms the system's existence. Both the biblical and historical records depict the collapse of the Gentile empire system — the defeat of a satanic attempt at world control. Its demise directly resulted from the first coming of Jesus and the establishing of the true Church. Daniel 2:34,35,44 spells this out clearly.

The stone of Nebuchadnezzar's dream is a type of Christ. During the Roman Empire, the Father sent Jesus Who struck a death blow to Satan's system and established His kingdom, the Church, upon the earth.

John states that the system will be restored briefly, then totally destroyed.

> "...And those who dwell on the earth will marvel, whose names are not written in the Book of Life from the foundation of the world, when they see the beast that was, and is not, and yet is.
>
> "Here is the mind which has wisdom: The seven heads are seven mountains on which the woman sits. There are also seven kings. Five have fallen, one is, and the other has not yet come. And when he comes, he must continue a short time" (vv. 8-10).

This statement, **The seven heads are seven mountains on which the woman sits** (v. 9), is easily explained. We know that each of the seven crowned heads represents a great kingdom. Verse 9 confirms this.

In examining the word *mountain*, we use a law of interpretation established by God's Word. When **mountain** is used in a passage which does not specifically name an existing range of mountains for a geographical location, it represents a kingdom. By reading the verses above and below the one in which **mountain** is used, you discover that it refers to a kingdom, not to a pile of dirt and rocks. The seven heads of verse 9 are seven great kingdoms. Verse 10 further confirms this: **There are also seven kings.** A king, a national leader, is over each of the seven kingdoms.

When John states **five have fallen,** he refers to the past. History records that at the time John received this prophecy, five great Gentile empires had come and gone. He also said, **...one is** (the sixth), **and the other** (the seventh one) **has not yet come.**

On which the woman sits indicates that the woman has tremendously influenced each of the kingdoms over a vast period of time.

The Seven Kingdoms

History names the great kingdoms or Gentile empires that the heads of the Beast System represent. The first is the Babylonian or Egyptian Empire; the second, the Assyrian; the third, the great Babylonian Empire under Nebuchadnezzar and his grandson, Belshazzar.

When Israel began to fall away from God, the first great Gentile empire to form was the Assyrian. The Babylonians then overthrew the Assyrian Empire by dissolving it into their own. At the time of the Babylonian Empire, Daniel began his prophecies concerning the development of the Gentile empires. Also, Judah and Benjamin, the last two tribes of Israel, were taken captive.

The fourth head was the Medo-Persian Empire. Daniel 5:5-31 records the account of the handwriting that appeared on the wall. It told of the Babylonian Empire's destruction and the rise of the Medes and the Persians. This fourth empire gave way to the fifth, the Greek Empire under Alexander the Great. When it collapsed, the sixth, the Roman Empire, swallowed it up.

The Roman Empire existed when John received the prophecy. During this time Jesus came to earth, laid the foundation for His Church and became its Chief

Cornerstone. The apostles began building on that foundation. The Church would accomplish an extremely productive work during its approximately 2,000 years on earth between the sixth and seventh heads of the system. The coming of Jesus Christ struck Satan a tremendous mortal blow. The Beast System collapsed with the fall of the Roman Empire.

Examining these biblical and historical truths gives us good understanding of what God is doing. As long as the Church is on the earth carrying out Jesus' ministry, the system cannot return to full operation. We are presently watching the system being prefabricated. After the Church is caught up, the Antichrist will fit the pieces together. This will be the resurrection of the system which produced the sixth head that was wounded unto death, the Roman Empire.

The vast Satan-motivated Gentile system had three major divisions: government, commerce and religion. When one empire succeeded another, the head of government changed, but the commercial and religious systems remained the same. Religions were always controlled by witchcraft in its most cunning and subtle form, commanding control of the people. As a sum total of the previous five heads, the Roman Empire was very wicked, immoral and pagan.

The Church is a godly vehicle; the empire system, satanic. Because the Church has the greatest power and authority, the satanic system cannot operate as long as the Church is on earth.

The Seventh and Eighth Heads

Numerous attempts have been made to restore the system; Napoleon, Hitler and Mussolini were only three of many who tried, though unsuccessfully. For the first time since the fall of the Roman Empire, today's events clearly expose initial groundwork being laid for the restoration of the system. We identify the Common Market of Europe, or the European Economic Community, an amalgamation of twelve states, with the embryo stage of development. Watch this system closely.

The resurrected system — the seventh head — will not be a restoration of the Roman Empire but of the system that produced the Roman Empire. It will be comprised of a *minimum* of ten nations and will not necessarily be contained in the same geographical area as the Roman Empire.[1]

In January of 1972 England, Ireland, Norway and Denmark signed documents to join the Common Market, suddenly bringing its membership to ten nations. When God put it in the hearts of the Norwegians to reject membership, they failed to ratify their treaty. The Common Market dropped from ten nations to nine. This action delayed the formation of the seventh head until Greece became the tenth member on January 1, 1981. Presently there are twelve members of the Common Market. Spain and Portugal were the last to be admitted. However, several applications now await approval, including that of Switzerland. The nations of the Common Market will bring forth the Antichrist once the Church is caught away.

Of verse 9 we can only conclude that **seven mountains** refer to the seven great kingdoms, each ruled by a king. Today, six of them have fallen. The seventh head, now in its infancy, will produce the eighth head, the Antichrist. Remember that the little horn of Daniel, chapters 7 and 8, is the same as the "eighth head" of Revelation 17:11. Both symbols identify the Antichrist.

According to John, once the seventh head becomes operational under the Antichrist, it lasts only a short time (the first three-and-one-half years of the Tribulation). During this time, the Antichrist brings together the

---

[1]Daniel 7:8 shows the Antichrist uproots three of the original nations. This indicates that the Common Market will be comprised of more than ten nations in order to maintain a membership of ten after a loss of three.

governments, armies, commerce and religions of the ten-nation confederacy. He uses the harlot system to advance himself to the center of world religion.

At mid-Tribulation the Antichrist, produced by the seventh head, assumes the identity of the eighth head. **The beast that was, and is not, is himself also the eighth, and is of the seven...** (v. 11). He attempts to force himself on the world as a self-appointed "god," existing for only three-and-one-half years before being totally destroyed when Christ returns.

> **The ten horns which you saw are ten kings who have received no kingdom as yet, but they receive authority for one hour as kings with the beast. These are of one mind, and they will give their power and authority to the beast. These** (the ten kings) **will make war with the Lamb** (Jesus)... (vv. 12-14).

The ten kings of the ten nations enter into a strong agreement with the Antichrist, pledging him their armies and their influence. Upon the anticipated success of the Antichrist's campaign, the kings will receive great kingdoms.

This is the alliance of rulers and armies which the Antichrist leads on the final day of the Tribulation. The combined armies of the kings are destroyed in the Battle of Armageddon fought against the returning Christ.

In the scene of verse 14 — Christ's return to the earth — we are given further proof that the Church is caught up before the Tribulation's final day:

> **...and the Lamb will overcome them, for He is Lord of lords and King of kings; and those who are with Him are called, chosen, and faithful.**

Throughout the New Testament the terms **called**, **chosen** and **faithful** identify members of the true Church — the Body of Christ. The **called, chosen, and faithful** —

the Church company — is returning with Jesus. (Zech. 14:5 also confirms this truth.) The members of the Church will administrate Jesus' kingdom on earth.

The Destruction of the Harlot

When the Antichrist is ready to pursue his ambition to become God, he must destroy the religious system in order to rule unopposed as the spiritual leader. The following passage describes the destruction of the harlot religious system:

> Then he said to me, "The waters which you saw, where the harlot sits, are peoples, multitudes, nations, and tongues. And the ten horns which you saw on the beast, these will hate the harlot, make her desolate and naked, eat her flesh and burn her with fire" (vv. 15,16).

Hating the influence of the harlot upon their people, the Antichrist and the False Prophet use the military power of the ten nations to quickly destroy her. The national leaders happily accommodate, because the harlot has been a great irritation to them.

Notice that God put it in the hearts of the ten kings to destroy the harlot. This action gives us insight into God's sovereignty. We see another example of God's use of the Egyptian pharaoh described in the following passage:

> And I will harden Pharaoh's heart, and multiply My signs and My wonders in the land of Egypt. But Pharaoh will not heed you, so that I may lay My hand on Egypt and bring My armies and My people, the children of Israel, out of the land of Egypt by great judgments.
>
> **Exodus 7:3,4**

Sovereign means "above all others, chief, supreme in power, ruler, independent of all others." The pharaoh was already against Israel. God simply strengthened or hardened his attitude all the more. The same was true of the ten kings. God put within them (or gave them over to) their desires.

Both the pharaoh and the kings had a choice. Since they decided to pursue evil, God allowed them to become totally driven by those desires. God's sovereignty extends even to withholding His restraint. He allows those who have evil intentions to carry them out. In one case, God used His sovereignty directly for the good of Israel; in the other, He used it to destroy part of Satan's operation. Again, the outcome was for the ultimate good of the people.

At the Antichrist's right hand is the False Prophet who, of course, gives his approval for the harlot's destruction. The followers of the Beast System accept their leaders' decision. The harlot's destruction clears the way for the False Prophet to announce the implementation of the mark of the Beast and worship of his image.

From the temple in Jerusalem, the Antichrist starts exerting his influence. These mid-Tribulation events prepare the way of the Antichrist for the next three-and-one-half years.

The Destroyed City

> **For God has put it in their hearts to fulfill His purpose, to be of one mind, and to give their kingdom to the beast, until the words of God are fulfilled.**
>
> **And the woman whom you saw is that great city which reigns over the kings of the earth (vv. 17,18).**

There have been several theories as to the identity of the city which is destroyed. All of them are pure speculation. Some people reason that the city of Babylon will be rebuilt and repopulated. Others suggest Rome, Italy.

Many years ago some theologians taught that the **seven mountains on which the woman sits** are the seven hills of Rome. They concluded that the Roman Catholic Church is the harlot. This is not so!

164

The harlot is not any single denominational structure. She is an amalgamation of *all* the world's ecclesiastical, man-made religions, including the present-day denominations choosing to have only a form of godliness.

Today the ancient harlot is about to receive a new vehicle through which she can function. Quite possibly it is the World Council of Churches, which works for unity of all religions. While man-made religions are working to bring all Christians under their control, the Holy Spirit is working to bring them together as the glorious Church!

We know the city destroyed at mid-Tribulation will be the headquarters of the harlot religious system or, as some have identified it, the world church. But its exact identity is unknown. Presently it is Geneva, Switzerland, headquarters of the World Council of Churches, World Bank center and city of treaties between nations.

Instead of being sidetracked with the Beast's different facets, we need to view the system as a whole. Just remember: its major parts are presently being prefabricated and it will be an amazing man who brings together into one operation these pieces of governments, commerce, armies and the harlot religious system.

15

Revelation 14 and 15 Informational

The first five verses of Revelation 14 continue the description of the 144,000 Jewish evangelists begun in Revelation 7. Since we have already examined this information, we will begin our study with verse 6.

The Angels' Ministry

Angels minister to all nations during the last half of the Tribulation.

> Then I saw another angel flying in the midst of heaven, having the everlasting gospel to preach to those who dwell on the earth — to every nation, tribe, tongue, and people — saying with a loud voice, "Fear God and give glory to Him, for the hour of His judgment has come; and worship Him who made heaven and earth, the sea and springs of water."
> **Revelation 14:6,7**

We learned from Revelation 5 that all the angels (approximately 100 billion) appear in heaven around God's throne at the sounding of His trumpet. At this time the Church company has been received from earth to heaven. Since the Scriptures give us insight into the assignment and ministry of angels, we know they will assist the 144,000 plus take up assignments in behalf of their converts.

At mid-Tribulation when the converts of the 144,000 Jewish evangelists are caught up, angels will again take up and carry out their earthly assignments. Their ministry runs concurrently with that of the Two Witnesses in Jerusalem and the Jewish evangelists to the remnant of Israel.

The Church is the present-day vehicle for preaching the Gospel. Once it finishes its assignment and is caught up, God selects the 144,000 Jewish evangelists to preach the Gospel. As the 144,000 are about to depart for heaven after finishing their assignment, the angels begin preaching the Gospel.

God's mercy endures forever. Through His divine order, He keeps the Gospel steadily flowing to all the earth. Salvation is still available through believing the Gospel, **the power of God to salvation** (Rom. 1:16).

"Worship God"

Proclaiming that the hour of God's judgment has come, angels call on people to fear and worship God, the glorious Creator of all.

As we have seen, this action creates an enormous problem for the Antichrist. It is obvious to the people he is attempting to influence that he cannot control the preaching angels (or the Two Witnesses or the plagues). This is only the beginning of his troubles.

"Babylon Is Fallen"

The angelic ministry is extremely diverse. While some angels are preaching the everlasting Gospel to all nations, others are announcing the destruction of the Babylonian harlot religious system.

> **And another angel followed, saying, "Babylon is fallen, is fallen, that great city, because she has made all nations drink of the wine of the wrath of her fornication"** (v. 8).

These angels announce to the world that the Antichrist led his armies in the harlot's destruction to make way for the fulfillment of his own evil ambition to become God.

"Do Not Take the Mark or Worship the Image of the Beast"

Then a third angel followed them, saying with a loud voice, "If anyone worships the beast and his image, and receives his mark on his forehead or on his hand, he himself shall also drink of the wine of the wrath of God, which is poured out full strength into the cup of His indignation.

"He shall be tormented with fire and brimstone in the presence of the holy angels and in the presence of the Lamb. And the smoke of their torment ascends forever and ever; and they have no rest day or night, who worship the beast and his image, and whoever receives the mark of his name."

Here is the patience of the saints; here are those who keep the commandments of God and the faith of Jesus (vv. 9-12).

Another angel warns against becoming involved with the Antichrist's new religion. The angels are actually saying, "With the destruction of the religious harlot, you are free from the bondage which controlled you through false religion!" (We learned of the harlot's widespread control in Rev. 17.)

As the angels inform the people of the harlot's destruction, they strongly warn against taking the mark of the Beast and worshiping his image. Through the angels, God further demonstrates His love by forewarning the people of the consequences: separation from God and eternal punishment in the lake of fire.

Literal Hell

Some people question the existence of a literal hell. They wonder whether there will be eternal punishment in an actual lake of fire. The infallible Scriptures teach that hell exists. The Bible is the only book which is absolutely accurate. God's Word is settled in heaven and He changes not. (Ps. 119:89; Mal. 3:6.)

Some scholars point out that no Greek word exists for the English word *everlasting*. The Greek word used, *aion*, means "age." An age has a beginning and an ending. Additionally, the Scripture uses "age upon age." In the original translations, one finds the use of *aion* upon *aion*, which simply means "ages unending."

In studying the whole biblical account, we discover that the same Greek word implying "everlasting punishment and torment" is used to indicate both the everlasting life of one who has accepted Jesus as Savior and the everlasting existence of God. If the Greek word *aion* does not imply everlasting punishment, it must not imply that God's existence is everlasting, an obviously invalid conclusion. Allow Scripture to interpret and support other Scripture.

"Church, Be Patient"

A strong admonition emerges from verse 12. By the Holy Spirit, John calls on the Church — of his day and ours — to be patient, to keep God's Word and their faith in Jesus. Refuse to be sidetracked and carried off by any wind of doctrine.

A Preview of the Battle of Armageddon

> Then I heard a voice from heaven saying to me, "Write: 'Blessed are the dead who die in the Lord from now on.'" "Yes," says the Spirit, "that they may rest from their labors, and their works follow them."
>
> Then I looked, and behold, a white cloud, and on the cloud sat One like the Son of Man, having on His head a golden crown, and in His hand a sharp sickle.
>
> And another angel came out of the temple, crying with a loud voice to Him who sat on the cloud, "Thrust in Your sickle and reap, for the time has come for You to reap, for the harvest of the earth is ripe."
>
> So He who sat on the cloud thrust in His sickle on the earth, and the earth was reaped (vv. 13-16).

The remainder of Revelation 14 previews the forthcoming Battle of Armageddon. Christ is pictured preparing to harvest the whole earth. This event involves His return when He takes over all governments.

> **And another angel came out from the altar, who had power over fire, and he cried with a loud cry to him who had the sharp sickle, saying, "Thrust in your sharp sickle and gather the clusters of the vine of the earth, for her grapes are fully ripe."**
>
> **So the angel thrust his sickle into the earth and gathered the vine of the earth, and threw it into the great winepress of the wrath of God. And the winepress was trampled outside the city, and the blood came out of the winepress, up to the horses' bridles, for one thousand six hundred furlongs[1] (vv. 18-20).**

The clusters of the vine of the earth are the earth's people. The winepress of this verse is the same as the one of God in Revelation 19:15. Jesus' action of treading the winepress symbolizes His destroying the Antichrist's evil forces at Armageddon.

The preview of the final battle continues. Armies from many areas of the world — particularly Europe, the Mediterranean and the Orient — converge at the battle site. Jesus returns to earth. At that moment, Jesus speaks the Word while standing on the Mount of Olives. This releases the plague vividly described in Zechariah 14:12. In one hour, the vast armada of hundreds of millions is reduced to a pool of blood filling an area of approximately 200 miles. Revelation 19 describes the Battle of Armageddon in greater detail.

Introduction to the
Tribulation's Final Month

Revelation 15 serves as an introduction to Revelation 16, an especially important chapter which brings the intense

---

[1] A furlong is 1/8 of a mile or 220 yards. *Sixteen hundred furlongs* equals 352,000 yards; 1,760 yards equals one mile; thus 1,600 furlongs equals 200 miles.

story into its final month. The following passage describes the severity of the last seven plagues released during this month, which continue to the Battle of Armageddon, and the magnitude of the events about to occur:

> **Then I saw another sign in heaven, great and marvelous: seven angels having the seven last plagues, for in them the wrath of God is complete. And I saw something like a sea of glass mingled with fire, and those who have the victory over the beast, over his image and over his mark and over the number of his name, standing on the sea of glass, having harps of God.**
> **Revelation 15:1,2**

Verse 2 contains the second reference to the crystal sea John sees before the great throne of God. Throughout the Scriptures, fire is a type of symbolism of the Holy Spirit at work. The crystal sea (the Church company) **mingled with fire** is the product of the Holy Spirit's activities. Many other people are supported by the Church, indicating the tremendous importance of the Church's position, especially the relationship between the Church and the natural seed of Israel as set forth by Paul in Romans 11.

John also describes those people, victorious over the Antichrist and his system, (including the Jewish evangelists and their converts) caught up during the Tribulation.

> **They sing the song of Moses, the servant of God, and the song of the Lamb, saying: "Great and marvelous are Your works, Lord God Almighty! Just and true are Your ways, O King of the saints!"** (v. 3).

The **King of the saints** is Jesus. We saw that according to Zechariah 8:23 many Gentiles are saved during the Tribulation.[2] However, the Great Multitude is basically an Israeli company, just as the first group taken up to heaven, the Church, is basically Gentile.

---

[2]Zechariah 8:23 correlates with Revelation 7:9-17, the description of the Great Multitude's catching up at mid-Tribulation.

> Who shall not fear You, O Lord, and glorify Your name? For You alone are holy. For all nations shall come and worship before You, for Your judgments have been manifested (v. 4).

Continuing its worship in song before the throne, this group gives an accurate account of the scenes of worship which will occur during Jesus' 1,000-year reign on earth. All nations, righteous or not, will come and worship before the Lamb. (See Zech. 14:16.)

> After these things I looked, and behold, the temple of the tabernacle of the testimony in heaven was opened. And out of the temple came the seven angels having the seven plagues, clothed in pure bright linen, and having their chests girded with golden bands.
>
> Then one of the four living creatures gave to the seven angels seven golden bowls full of the wrath of God who lives forever and ever.
>
> The temple was filled with smoke from the glory of God and from His power, and no one was able to enter the temple till the seven plagues of the seven angels were completed (vv. 5-8).

The way for the last plagues is now prepared!

PART V
The Prophecy
Revelation 16, 18-20

16
Revelation 16
Earth
The Seven Last Plagues

Many years ago when I first began teaching Revelation 16, I saw no time frame associated with the plagues it describes. I went to prayer. "Father, someone is eventually going to ask me how long these plagues last, and I'll have to say, 'I don't know.' If there is anything in Your Word that will help me understand how long they last, please call it to my attention."

My Father answered by asking, "Is this the first time I have ever used plagues to deliver the children of Israel?"

"No," I replied. "You used plagues once before when the Israelis were in Egyptian bondage."

When He urged me to read that account, I knew He was about to give me good insight. Immediately, I read Exodus 7 through 12, the story of the ten plagues under Moses' direction, which God used to deliver Israel out of bondage. The plagues began and ended in the course of one month. This suggests that the plagues of Revelation begin during the Tribulation's final month. Because of the devastating nature of these plagues, it is not likely that they last for a full month, but will continue to the time of Christ's return and the Battle of Armageddon.

In the Exodus account, there are ten plagues, beginning and ending in a single month; in Revelation, only seven.

However, with the exception of the passing over of the death angel, the nature of the Revelation plagues is far more hideous than the Exodus plagues. Were these plagues to last a month, no one on whom they were poured could survive. God does not bring this sinful generation to such an end. These last seven plagues are designed to aid in the destruction of the Babylonian Beast System, the Antichrist and the False Prophet. Due to the horrible nature of these plagues, they begin only days before the final day of the Tribulation.

A Grievous Sore

> Then I heard a loud voice from the temple saying to the seven angels, "Go and pour out the bowls of the wrath of God on the earth." So the first went and poured out his bowl upon the earth, and a foul and loathsome sore came upon the men who had the mark of the beast and those who worshiped his image (vv. 1,2).

The first plague is a noisome and grievous sore, like a horrible boil, which brings severe suffering from infection and fever. The final plagues, released as direct wrath from God, fall on the wicked. Notice that the first plague affects *only* those people who have taken the mark of the Beast and worshiped his image! This indicates that people who have refused to take the mark of the Beast survive.[1]

The Waters Become Blood

> Then the second angel poured out his bowl on the sea, and it became blood as of a dead man; and every living creature in the sea died (v. 3).

---

[1]Many people survive the Tribulation. (See Isa. 19:23-25; Zech. 14:18,19; Rev. 12:14.) They will have refused to take the mark of the Beast or worship his image, and will have lived through wars and plagues. This will not be easy, but man has a great asset: the determination to survive.

The plague released by the second trumpet of Revelation, chapter 8, causes one-third of the seas to become blood.[2] With the plague released by the second vial of Revelation, chapter 16, the remaining two-thirds of the seas become as blood. This blood is like the thick, coagulated blood of a dead man which gives off a great stench! Immediately, all ships afloat sink and all aboard drown in this blood. How horrible!

Then the third angel poured out his bowl on the rivers and springs of water, and they became blood (v. 4).

The blood of the third plague is the type that flows when one is cut severely.

And I heard the angel of the waters saying: "You are righteous, O Lord, the One who is and who was and who is to be, because You have judged these things. For they have shed the blood of saints and prophets, and You have given them blood to drink. For it is their just due" (vv. 5,6).

Giving the wicked blood to drink is a just punishment. Many of them shed the blood of the apostles and saints.

And I heard another from the altar saying, "Even so, Lord God Almighty, true and righteous are Your judgments" (v. 7).

The people under the altar are the martyred saints of the Tribulation. (Rev. 6.) Apparently aware of what is happening, they proclaim, "You are perfectly just in dealing this way with the rebellious people."

As the third trumpet sounds, one-third of the sources of domestic water becomes poisoned. The seas and sources of domestic waters are partially affected by the second and third plagues of Revelation 8. The pouring of the second

---

[2]The seas which are turned into blood are the Mediterranean Sea and waters around Europe, the seat of the Antichrist. Not all large bodies of water will be smitten.

and third vials of Revelation 16 completes these two plagues of Revelation 8, affecting a large percentage of the waters on earth. In the remainder of the Tribulation's last month, followers of the Antichrist have no source of water. They can only quench their thirst with blood.[3]

Unrepentant Hearts

Then the fourth angel poured out his bowl on the sun, and power was given to him to scorch men with fire. And men were scorched with great heat, and they blasphemed the name of God who has power over these plagues; and they did not repent and give Him glory (vv. 8,9).

As the fourth trumpet sounds, the sun, moon and stars are darkened, giving no natural light for an eight-hour period of each day. The plague released by the pouring of the fourth vial affects the sun, causing it to give forth extremely hot rays. Men suffer heat prostration, severe sunburn and dehydration.

Then the fifth angel poured out his bowl on the throne of the beast, and his kingdom became full of darkness; and they gnawed their tongues because of the pain (v. 10).

The seat of the Beast is in the geographical area that comes under the Antichrist's authority. Prophetic Scriptures reveal this to be basically the European-Mediterranean area. The pouring of the fifth vial brings darkness upon the Antichrist's entire kingdom. This completes the plague begun by the sounding of the fourth trumpet. No natural light shines over the nations under the Beast System.

With the immense suffering occurring, one would think that repentance would be universal. The reverse is true —

---

[3]The plague causing domestic waters to become blood is not worldwide. Remember, the remnant of Israel is still hidden among other people somewhere on earth.

people blaspheme God all the more because of their suffering.

They blasphemed the God of heaven because of their pains and their sores, and did not repent of their deeds (v. 11).

The Armies Gather

The pouring of the sixth vial directly relates to the sounding of the sixth trumpet of Revelation 9.

Then the sixth angel poured out his bowl on the great river Euphrates, and its water was dried up, so that the way of the kings from the east might be prepared (v. 12).

The sixth trumpet releases the vast demon-driven Oriental army. To reach its destination, the battle sight of Armageddon, it marches through the Asian areas, destroying everything in its path.

And I saw three unclean spirits like frogs coming out of the mouth of the dragon, out of the mouth of the beast, and out of the mouth of the false prophet. For they are spirits of demons, performing signs, which go out to the kings of the earth and of the whole world, to gather them to the battle of that great day of God Almighty (vv. 13,14).

The battle of that great day of God Almighty is the Battle of Armageddon! Satan is the dragon gathering as many armies as possible. He must use man in his last futile effort to defeat the Lord Jesus.

The following statement refers to Jesus' appearing to receive the Church. This places the Church company on the winning side at Armageddon. Carefully read this admonition from Jesus:

"Behold, I am coming as a thief. Blessed is he who watches, and keeps his garments, lest he walk naked and they see his shame."

> **And they gathered them together to the place called in Hebrew, Armageddon** (vv. 15,16).

Many major battles have been fought in the Valley of Megiddo that stretches into the great plains of the Valley of Jezreel. This sight is used again for the Battle of Armageddon.

Nature's Final Upheaval

> **Then the seventh angel poured out his bowl into the air, and a loud voice came out of the temple of heaven, from the throne, saying, "It is done!"** (v. 17).

As the Tribulation comes to an end, the seventh angel pours his vial into the air as the pronouncement comes from heaven, **It is done!** This signals the sounding of the seventh trumpet. This is the same event as the angel's declaration in Revelation 10:7:

> **But in the days of the sounding of the seventh angel, when he is about to sound, the mystery of God would be finished, as He declared to His servants the prophets.**

Suddenly the most tremendous upheaval of nature ever to occur begins. This is the cataclysmic event which follows Jesus' opening of the sixth seal (Rev. 6) and the sounding of the final trumpet (Rev. 11).

> **And there were noises and thunderings and lightnings; and there was a great earthquake, such a mighty and great earthquake as had not occurred since men were on earth.**
>
> **Now the great city was divided into three parts, and the cities of the nations fell. And great Babylon was remembered before God, to give her the cup of the wine of the fierceness of His wrath.**
>
> **Then every island fled away, and the mountains were not found.**
>
> **And great hail from heaven fell upon men, every hailstone about the weight of a talent. Men blasphemed**

God because of the plague of the hail, since that plague was exceedingly great (vv. 18-21).

When the seventh and last angelic trumpet sounds, a series of events occur on the final day of the Tribulation, as recorded in Revelation 6:12-17; 11:15-18; and 16:17-21. On the final day of the Tribulation, chaotic, cataclysmic, devastating, awesome and supernatural events occur. A combination of the sixth seal, seventh trumpet and seventh vial of God's wrath are enacted in a twenty-four-hour period. Allow me to categorize and list these events.

1. **Upheaval of Nature.**

   A. Great earthquake. (Rev. 6:12; 11:19; 16:18.)

   B. Sun becomes black, moon as blood. (Rev. 6:12; Joel 2:28-31; Matt. 24:29.)

   C. Stars fall, collide with earth. (Rev. 6:13.)

   D. Sky recedes, rolls up. (Rev. 6:14; 19:11.)

   E. Mountains moved. (Rev. 6:14; 16:20.)

   F. Islands moved. (Rev. 6:14; 16:20.)

   G. Thunderings and lightnings. (Rev. 11:19; 16:18.)

   H. Hailstorm. (Rev. 11:19; 16:21.)

2. **Destruction.**

   A. Earth struck severe blow by falling stars (Rev. 6:13); should fulfill Isaiah 13:13.

   B. Jerusalem divided into three parts. (Rev. 16:19.)

   C. Cities around the world destroyed. (Rev. 16:19.)

   D. Godless Babylonian Beast System used by the Antichrist destroyed. (Rev. 16:19.)

   E. Armageddon. (First and last statements of Rev. 11:18; also Rev. 19:11-21 and Zech. 14.)

3. Supernatural Action.

A. Kingdoms of world become kingdoms of our Lord. (Isa. 9:6; Rev. 11:15,17; 19:11-21.)

B. Righteous dead — martyrs — are resurrected and judged. (This is a righteous judgment — a good one!) (Rev. 11:18.)

C. Rewarding of the prophets (Two Witnesses) and Tribulation saints. (Rev. 11:18.)

D. Men of all ranks attempt to hide from God. (Rev. 6:15,16.)

E. Jesus and His army of saints return to defeat Satan, the Antichrist and the False Prophet. (Zech. 14; Rev. 6:17; 19:11-20.)

God remembers **Babylon**, the total Babylonian Beast System used by the Antichrist, and pours out the fierceness of His wrath. The upheaval is so devastating that the entire surface of the earth changes. As the earthquake destroys the land, hail weighing a talent (approximately 120 pounds) falls from heaven. This upheaval could easily bring about the fulfillment of Isaiah 13:13 which states, **The earth will move out of her place.** Such an event would correct the earth's axis.

Imagine the terrible scene. The stench of the oceans' coagulated blood fills the atmosphere. The rays of the sun are hot, and no water is available to drink — only blood! The people who have taken the mark of the Beast and worshiped his image are troubled with boils and, of course, raging fever. On this final day of the Tribulation, people are suffering from the last plagues, the great earthquake and hailstones, the return of Christ to the earth and the monumental Battle of Armageddon.

This horrible scene results from the sin of rebellion against God. **There is a way that seems right to a man, but** its end is the way of death (Prov. 14:12). Rejection of Jesus Christ, combined with the stubbornness of following selfish desires, causes multitudes of people to be destroyed by the fruit of their devices. Jesus said, **I am the way, the truth, and the life. No one comes to the Father except through Me** (John 14:6). Living through the horror of the Tribulation's final month can be avoided by accepting Jesus.

As you have examined all the events which are to occur on the last day of the Tribulation, I am sure you noticed that there is not even a hint of a great catching up among them. Only the Two Witnesses of Revelation 11:11-13 are taken up on that day. It is a day of returning to the earth for Jesus, the Church, the 144,000 and the mid-Tribulation company, who were also caught away from earth to heaven.

17

Revelation 18 and 19 Informational/Heaven and Earth

The Harlot's Obituary

The coming together of the harlot religious company fulfills Paul's prophecy concerning a spiritual falling away, which precedes the emergence of the Antichrist and the False Prophet.

> Let no one deceive you by any means; for that Day will not come unless the falling away comes first, and the man of sin is revealed, the son of perdition.
> **2 Thessalonians 2:3**

The Antichrist's mid-Tribulation destruction of the harlot church clears the way for his doomed attempt to become the worldwide religious leader. Revelation 18 is the harlot's obituary.

In the following verse God calls His people to withdraw from the harlot:

> And I heard another voice from heaven saying, "Come out of her, my people, lest you share in her sins, and lest you receive of her plagues."
> **Revelation 18:4**

Within the world's religious orders are many God-fearing men and women who have no desire to be part of a harlot church. The Holy Spirit warns these people of the danger and pleads with them to draw away from these religious organizations determinedly moving from God.

Consider Paul's statement concerning those people **having a form of godliness, but denying the power thereof:** *from such turn away* (2 Tim. 3:5 KJV).

The harlot is responsible for **the blood of prophets and saints, and of all who were slain on the earth** (Rev. 18:24). This includes those people killed during wars. This religious system is so evil that God puts the desire to utterly destroy her in the hearts of the ten kings. Apparently nuclear weapons are used — the harlot, her city and perhaps multitudes of people are totally destroyed in one hour. Never again will there be events of life in that city.

The harlot is so rich and influential that men who are controlled by the love of money mourn when she is destroyed. They weep and refuse to approach the city's fearful site.

Heaven at Mid-Tribulation

The description of heaven rejoicing over the destruction of the harlot places the opening events of Revelation 19 after mid-Tribulation.

> After these things I heard a loud voice of a great multitude in heaven, saying, "Alleluia! Salvation and glory and honor and power to the Lord our God! For true and righteous are His judgments, because He has judged the great harlot who corrupted the earth with her fornication; and He has avenged on her the blood of His servants shed by her." Again they said, "Alleluia! Her smoke rises up forever and ever!"
>
> And the twenty-four elders and the four living creatures fell down and worshiped God who sat on the throne, saying, "Amen! Alleluia!"
>
> Then a voice came from the throne, saying, "Praise our God, all you His servants and those who fear Him, both small and great!"
>
> And I heard, as it were, the voice of a great multitude, as the sound of many waters and as the

sound of mighty thunderings, saying, "Alleluia! For the Lord God Omnipotent reigns! Let us be glad and rejoice and give Him glory, for the marriage of the Lamb has come, and His wife has made herself ready."

And to her it was granted to be arrayed in fine linen, clean and bright, for the fine linen is the righteous acts of the saints.

Then he said to me, "Write: 'Blessed are those who are called to the marriage supper of the Lamb!'" And he said to me, "These are the true sayings of God."

Revelation 19:1-9

The story developing around God's throne continues.[1] Heaven is the site of the Marriage of the Lamb and Marriage Supper. An enormous number of people in heaven offer statements of praise, thanksgiving and glory to God, revealing His judgments to be righteous. He judged the great harlot, which corrupted the earth with her fornications, and avenged His servants' blood which she shed. This praise and worship is also preparation for the Marriage of the Lamb.

The group worshiping at God's throne is composed of the Church company, the Great Multitude and the 144,000 Jewish evangelists. From the information given to us in Revelation 14:1-5, we can properly place the 144,000 Jewish evangelists in the heavenly scene.

After the 144,000 finish their assignment, Jesus meets them at Mount Zion to escort them to heaven. Mount Zion is a location both on earth and in heaven. (Heb. 12:22-24.) Jesus meets the 144,000 on the earthly Zion in Jerusalem. Because the 144,000 are part of the group worshiping before God's throne, described in verses 1-3, we know that Jesus escorts them to heaven. Remember, we interpret literally unless figures of speech or types are used within the context.

---

[1]Notice that the events described are heavenly, not earthly. The Church will have been caught up long before. (See Luke 21:36; Rev. 4:1,2; Heb. 9:28; 12:22-24; John 14:3; Titus 2:13; 2 Thess. 2:3,6-8.)

The 144,000 are still on earth during the five months of the plague of locusts. (Rev. 9.) From this we know it is after at least four years of the Tribulation that they are raptured. Once in heaven they join the Church company already there and together sing the new song of the redeemed! Chronologically, this places the Wedding and Wedding Supper after mid-Tribulation.

John declares what a blessed time this is in heaven: **Blessed are those who are called to the marriage supper of the Lamb!...These are the true sayings of God** (v. 9).

Man's Limited Knowledge

We can accept the information recorded in the Scriptures as the absolute **true sayings of God** without making an exhaustive study. Such a study on any portion of God's Word is impossible, because no human possesses total knowledge.

If man had total knowledge, he would think himself God, causing great trouble. God chose to share limited knowledge with man, giving each of His ministers a special insight into His Word. Everyone should have a general working knowledge of the Word with at least one area of special interest.

The Spirit of Prophecy

> And I fell at his feet to worship him. But he said to me, "See that you do not do that! I am your fellow servant, and of your brethren who have the testimony of Jesus. Worship God! For the testimony of Jesus is the spirit of prophecy" (v. 10).

John closes this portion of his description of heaven's future events with this: **...the testimony of Jesus is the spirit of prophecy.** Discovering this statement helped me in understanding part of Paul's teachings concerning the gift of prophecy. (See 1 Cor. 12.) Paul indicates that all may prophesy, but individually and in order. (1 Cor. 14.)

The testimony of Jesus is the spirit of prophecy. Every born-again believer has the testimony of Jesus. By sharing his delightful experience, he is setting forth an example, or prophesying, of what can happen to the hearer. So when one shares his personal testimony, the spirit of prophecy comes upon him.

Heaven and Earth at Jesus' Return

Verse 11 begins a transition from heaven back to earth. In the remainder of the chapter both stories are combined.

The White Horse Rider

Now I saw heaven opened, and behold, a white horse. And He who sat on him was called Faithful and True, and in righteousness He judges and makes war (v. 11).

This verse describes the Lord Jesus riding a white horse in His return to earth. Although the personal identity of the Revelation 6 white horse rider is cloaked, we know that he will become the Antichrist. The Revelation 19 white horse rider is easily identifiable as Jesus. He is **called Faithful and True, and in righteousness He judges and makes war.**

This statement that our God of love makes war surprises many people. An examination of God's Word reveals that He has made war on several occasions. God's nature is not only one of unfailing love, but of fierce indignation, fury and jealousy. He firmly allows no acquittal of the wicked and is a God of vengeance.

Study the Scriptures to examine every aspect of God's character. Even though God's major characteristic is love, especially toward those who want His love, He is well-rounded.

God delights in being our Father and friend. It is much better to meet Him in His love than in His wrath.

The Evil Armies' Destruction

The description of Jesus continues:

> His eyes were like a flame of fire, and on His head were many crowns. He had a name written that no one knew except Himself. He was clothed with a robe dipped in blood, and His name is called The Word of God. And the armies in heaven, clothed in fine linen, white and clean, followed Him on white horses.
>
> Now out of His mouth goes a sharp sword, that with it He should strike the nations. And He Himself will rule them with a rod of iron. He Himself treads the winepress of the fierceness and wrath of Almighty God (vv. 12-15).

The winepress of the above passage is the same one of Revelation 14:19,20. Jesus treads the winepress, destroying the Antichrist's evil forces at Armageddon.

> And He has on His robe and on His thigh a name written: KING OF KINGS AND LORD OF LORDS (v. 16).

Verses 12-16 contain a magnificent description of Jesus' literal return to earth. He stands upon the Mount of Olives, and using the two-edged Sword, God's Word, speaks into existence the plague that destroys the vast armies. (Zech. 14:4,12.)

> Then I saw an angel standing in the sun; and he cried with a loud voice, saying to all the birds that fly in the midst of heaven, "Come and gather together for the supper of the great God, that you may eat the flesh of kings, the flesh of captains, the flesh of mighty men, the flesh of horses and of those who sit on them, and the flesh of all people, free and slave, both small and great."
>
> And I saw the beast, the kings of the earth, and their armies, gathered together to make war against Him who sat on the horse and against His army.
>
> Then the beast was captured, and with him the

false prophet who worked signs in his presence, by which he deceived those who received the mark of the beast and those who worshiped his image. These two were cast alive into the lake of fire burning with brimstone.

And the rest were killed with the sword which proceeded from the mouth of Him who sat on the horse. And all the birds were filled with their flesh (vv. 17-21).

The fowls of the air are called to clean up the battlefield. This ends the Battle of Armageddon, which takes only one hour.

Jesus walks from the Mount of Olives through the little Valley of Kidron and onto the temple mount to assume control of all governments. (Isa. 9:6.)[2] He is proclaimed Lord of lords, King of kings and the Prince of Peace. (Zech. 14 also clearly depicts Jesus as King and Lord.) Then He begins His wonderful 1,000-year reign of peace and righteousness on earth. The Antichrist and False Prophet are cast alive into the lake of fire to begin their eternal punishment.

[2]Although Scriptures do not specifically state that Jesus will be proclaimed King on the temple mount, no other place is more suitable. Solomon and Zerubbabel built temples on Mount Moriah, and the future temple of Zechariah 6 must be in the same location. This site is revered by nearly all Jews. Jesus was no exception. He often was either on the Mount of Olives overlooking the temple mount or in Jerusalem on the temple mount.

18

Revelation 20
Earth and Heaven
The Millennium

Revelation 20 opens with the continuation of the earthly story, then with verse 11 returns to the heavenly scene.

Satan Imprisoned

Then I saw an angel coming down from heaven, having the key to the bottomless pit and a great chain in his hand.

He laid hold of the dragon, that serpent of old, who is the Devil and Satan, and bound him for a thousand years; and he cast him into the bottomless pit, and shut him up, and set a seal on him, so that he should deceive the nations no more till the thousand years were finished. But after these things he must be released for a little while (vv. 1-3).

The above verse contains all scriptural terms used to identify the devil: **dragon, serpent, Satan** and **Devil**. After the Antichrist and False Prophet are cast into the lake of fire, a great strong angel (probably Michael) arrests and binds Satan.

No mercy is shown Satan. He fully deserves the punishment of being cast into the bottomless pit with a seal set upon him to secure his imprisonment. At the end of the thousand years, Satan is loosed for a short season. (We will examine the reason for Satan's brief release later in this chapter.) The time frame of his imprisonment corresponds with Christ's reign of peace and righteousness on earth.

The Saints Rule With Jesus

And I saw thrones, and they sat on them, and judgment was committed to them... (v. 4).

The above verse describes many occupied thrones! The members of the Church return with Jesus to administrate His earthly kingdom for one thousand years. The Church receives their assignments for future duties while in heaven around God's throne.

During this reign, a theocratic government exists, a perfect administration. There are no political parties, labor unions or police. All positions of authority, from the local level to the highest government official, are filled by the saints who have returned with Jesus. You or someone you know may be king of the United States!

An Era of Health and Peace

Satan's imprisonment almost negates his earthly operation. Since he is the only cause of death, sickness and temptation, these become almost nonexistent.

Longevity of life is restored to these natural people, who continue to reproduce children.

No more shall an infant from there live but a few days, nor an old man who has not fulfilled his days; for the child shall die one hundred years old, but the sinner being one hundred years old shall be accursed.
Isaiah 65:20

If one were to die 100 years old, that person would still be considered a child. Any death during the Millennium results from sin begun in unrighteous people before Satan's imprisonment and their failure to repent.

Peace extends to all animals. **The wolf also shall dwell with the lamb, the leopard shall lie down with the young goat, the calf and the young lion and the fatling together...** (Isa. 11:6). Any creatures turned natural enemies by Adam's fall are reconciled. Parents need not worry about their children. Even if a child should reach into the hole of a serpent, he will not be bitten.

> **...Then I saw the souls of those who had been beheaded for their witness to Jesus and for the word of God, who had not worshiped the beast or his image, and had not received his mark on their foreheads or on their hands. And they lived and reigned with Christ for a thousand years (v. 4).**

This verse describes the martyred saints of the Tribulation discovered when the fifth seal is opened. Resurrected on the first day of the Millennium, they take their place with the Lord's victorious company, fully avenged.

The Resurrection of the Wicked Dead

The wicked dead from the time of Adam are resurrected at the end of the 1,000 years of peace. At that time, God judges all the wicked at the Great White Throne Judgment.

During the Millennium, God continues reaching out to the survivors of the Tribulation who did not bow to the Antichrist. Rather than destroying them, God offers them salvation.[1] They live in peace and righteousness and multiply upon the earth. God gives all men every opportunity to receive Jesus, waiting until after the Millennium ends to judge the wicked.

The First Resurrection

> **But the rest of the dead did not live again until the thousand years were finished. This is the first resurrection (v. 5).**

[1]The nations of Revelation 21:24-26 are saved during the Millennium. We know this because no unrighteousness can carry over onto the new earth.

The first resurrection includes all the raptures, or translations (four), and all resurrections (three), except the resurrection of the wicked dead.

Before the Tribulation begins, the Church is caught up. This involves the resurrection of the dead in Christ and the catching up of the living Christians. These two acts form one major event. (1 Thess. 4:16-18.)

Next, at mid-Tribulation, the Great Multitude, the converts of the 144,000, are caught away to remove them from the path of the Antichrist's wrath. (Rev. 7:9-17.) When their ministry is completed about six months later, the 144,000 Jewish evangelists are taken up. (Rev. 14:1-5.)

On the final day of the Tribulation (also the first day of the Millennium) the Two Witnesses are resurrected and taken up. (Rev. 11:3-12.) Later in that day, the martyred Tribulation saints are resurrected. (Rev. 20:4.) The first resurrection is comprised of these seven distinct events.

Satan Is Released

Blessed and holy is he who has part in the first resurrection. Over such the second death has no power, but they shall be priests of God and of Christ, and shall reign with Him a thousand years.

Now when the thousand years have expired, Satan will be released from his prison and will go out to deceive the nations which are in the four corners of the earth, Gog and Magog, to gather them together to battle, whose number is as the sand of the sea.

They went up on the breadth of the earth and surrounded the camp of the saints and the beloved city. And fire came down from God out of heaven and devoured them.

The devil, who deceived them, was cast into the lake of fire and brimstone where the beast and the false prophet are. And they will be tormented day and night forever and ever (vv. 6-10).

The four horsemen of the Apocalypse destroy one-fourth of the earth's population, the 200 million-man Oriental army destroys another third, and the plagues also take a toll. At the Tribulation's end, approximately thirty-five to forty percent of the earth's population is still alive. These are the people over whom Jesus begins His reign. They must be cared for, ministered to and put back into a productive society. Jesus rules them with **a rod of iron** (Rev. 19:15), or firm authority.

Many nations are saved during the Millennium. (Rev. 21:24.) However, even those who are not saved must worship Jesus during this time. (Zech. 14:16,17.) The people who do not receive Jesus as Savior and Lord have an opportunity to follow Satan when he is released from the bottomless pit at the end of the 1,000-year period.

Satan goes about the earth to deceive as many nations as possible. When God restores the power of choice, Satan gathers a large following of people and leads them against the camp of the saints and the Holy City.

God sends fire from heaven to end this strange battle, moving so swiftly that it is as though the battle never actually occurs. Satan is again taken captive, then cast into the lake of fire where the Antichrist and False Prophet have been for 1,000 years. The only people left alive on the earth are the saints from all time periods, the righteous remnant of Israel and the nations saved during Christ's reign.

Do not confuse the terms *Gog* and *Magog* of Revelation 20 with their use in Ezekiel 38 and 39. In Ezekiel's prophecies Gog and Magog represent a great northern power identifiable as Russia from the geographical areas described. This prophecy of Ezekiel 38 began to be fulfilled with the restoration of the nation of Israel. The Gog and Magog of Revelation 20 are gathered together from all over the earth and are destroyed.

Why is Satan released from the bottomless pit? Our God is a just God; He releases Satan for a short span of time, perhaps a few weeks. Satan immediately begins to tempt the people who have lived during the reign of our Lord Jesus. Understand that from the time of Adam everyone has been tempted by Satan and given the opportunity to overcome him. Were Satan not released at the end of the Millennium to tempt those people (not the righteous Church), all those who had previously yielded to Satan and were lost could accuse God of being unjust.

The Great White Throne Judgment

With verse 11 the scene changes from earth to the throne room in heaven:

> Then I saw a great white throne and Him who sat on it, from whose face the earth and the heaven fled away. And there was found no place for them.
>
> And I saw the dead, small and great, standing before God, and books were opened. And another book was opened, which is the Book of Life. And the dead were judged according to their works, by the things which were written in the books.
>
> The sea gave up the dead who were in it, and Death and Hades delivered up the dead who were in them. And they were judged, each one according to his works.
>
> Then Death and Hades were cast into the lake of fire. This is the second death. And anyone not found written in the Book of Life was cast into the lake of fire (vv. 11-15).

In this final resurrection, the wicked dead of all ages are resurrected to stand before God's throne. No one is left on earth, and hell is emptied.

While this judgment is taking place in heaven, earth and the heavens surrounding earth are destroyed.

God, as Judge, sits on one side of the throne. He is

backed by angels and the righteous people of all ages: the Old and New Testament saints, the Tribulation saints, the nations saved during the Millennium and the godly angels.

Waiting to be judged on the other side are all nations which did not turn to God, slain during the Tribulation or at the Millennium's end, and the fallen angels. Paul refers to these angels in Jude 6: **And the angels who did not keep their proper domain, but left their own abode, He has reserved in everlasting chains under darkness for the judgment of the great day.** First Corinthians 6:3 clearly states that the angels who did not keep their first estate will be judged by you and me, the Church. God judges fallen mankind while we judge fallen angels at the Great White Throne Judgment.

A question has been asked based on First Corinthians 6:2. That question is: When do the saints judge the world? The answer is: during the millennial reign of Jesus. At that time the Church will be ruling the world under Jesus as kings and priests. With vested authority, we will judge the world.

God judges the unrighteous according to their works recorded in the book He opens. Afterwards, He assigns them to their final place of punishment, the lake of fire. This is the second death, a state of eternal death!

The righteous never see the second death. What little God's Word tells us about the lake of fire is enough to reveal that no person in his right mind would want to be part of it.

The New Heaven, New Earth and New Jerusalem

After the Great White Throne Judgment, God is ready to bring about the new heaven and earth, and New Jerusalem. At the end of the Millennium, no people remain on earth — the wicked are in the lake of fire, the righteous in heaven awaiting God's next great act.

Peter describes the destruction of the earth and its immediate heavens which takes place during the final judgment:

> But the day of the Lord will come as a thief in the night, in which the heavens will pass away with a great noise, and the elements will melt with fervent heat; both the earth and the works that are in it will be burned up.
>
> **2 Peter 3:10**

God creates a new earth surrounded by a new heaven where His kingdom continues forever.

PART VI
Prophecy and Cover Letter
Conclusion
New Heaven, New Earth,
New Jerusalem

19

Revelation 21
Informational

Revelation 21 opens with John's description of the new heaven, new earth and New Jerusalem. Containing no large bodies of water, the new earth is larger in land area than the former earth.

> Now I saw a new heaven and a new earth, for the first heaven and the first earth had passed away. Also there was no more sea. Then I, John, saw the holy city, New Jerusalem, coming down out of heaven from God, prepared as a bride adorned for her husband (vv. 1,2).

Only righteous people live on the new earth. The following verse categorizes the unrighteous people who will suffer eternally in the lake of fire:

> But the cowardly, unbelieving, abominable, murderers, sexually immoral, sorcerers, idolaters, and all liars shall have their part in the lake which burns with fire and brimstone, which is the second death (v. 8).

Each of the letters to the seven churches of Asia contains statements to the overcomer, as does the following passage. God has tremendous plans for the company of overcomers.

> And I heard a loud voice from heaven saying, "Behold, the tabernacle of God is with men, and He will dwell with them, and they shall be His people. God Himself will be with them and be their God.
>
> "And God will wipe away every tear from their eyes; there shall be no more death, nor sorrow, nor

crying. There shall be no more pain, for the former things have passed away."

Then He who sat upon the throne said, "Behold, I make all things new." And He said to me, "Write, for these words are true and faithful." And He said to me, "It is done! I am the Alpha and the Omega, the Beginning and the End. I will give of the fountain of the water of life freely to him who thirsts. He who overcomes shall inherit all things, and I will be his God and he shall be My son" (vv. 3-7).

The Bride of Christ

Then one of the seven angels who had the seven bowls filled with the seven last plagues came to me and talked with me, saying, "Come, I will show you the bride, the Lamb's wife" (v. 9).

Throughout generations, it has been generally accepted and taught that the Church is the Bride of Christ. Is this teaching true, or is it a major tradition without biblical support?

I ask in good faith that, before reaching your conclusion, you examine all the associated biblical references thoroughly, allowing the Scripture to speak for itself. This I have done, and I am satisfied.

There can be no argument as to the present identity of the Church. According to the apostle Paul, the Church is the Body of Christ, of which Christ is the Head. (See Col. 1:18; Rom. 12:5; Eph. 1:22,23; 4:11-16.)

Please keep in mind that the terms *Church* and *Body of Christ* are interchangeable throughout Scripture. Also remember that although Jesus laid the foundation for the Church (Rom. 15:20; 1 Cor. 3:10-12) and is the Foundation as well as the Chief Cornerstone (Eph. 2:20), it was the apostle Paul to whom the revelation of the Church was given. Paul clearly establishes himself as **an apostle to the Gentiles** (Rom. 11:13).

I have learned through this study the difference between *identity* and *relationship*. Too often, believers have confused the two. When they have a wrong identity, it isn't likely they will develop a proper relationship with Jesus.

For as long as I can remember, it has been said that the Church is the Bride of Christ. This teaching has been based on the following Scripture references: Matthew 25:1-13, John 3:29 and Ephesians 5:24-30. Notice that not one of the above references identifies the Church as the Bride of Christ. As a matter of fact, there is not one verse of Scripture which says the Church is the Bride.

What then must we conclude? Apparently the Church has been given an identity that is incorrect. This identity is based on assumption or what one may call a "type" or "shadow." It is true that there are many types and shadows in the Scripture from which we receive insight. However, doctrine cannot be established on types and shadows.

The teaching that the Church is the Bride of Christ has become a doctrine within the Body of Christ without strong or clear support. This teaching has been around for so many years that it has become traditional. Once a tradition has been established, it is difficult to remove. In fact, people will fight over their traditions. It is certainly reasonable that we would have extreme difficulty in questioning this traditional doctrine. How could so many men and women of God teach a tradition and overlook the soundness of the Word?

Perhaps an interpretation of Isaiah 54:5 has clouded our thinking. It says, **For your Maker is your husband.** There can be no mistake that God is the husband of the people of Israel as is so declared within that chapter. One could conclude that since God is married to Israel, then Jesus would take the Church as His Bride.

However, allow me to remind you that we are wrestling with identity versus relationship for the Church.

After serious study of all the Scriptures which seem to give the Church a "Bride identity," I discovered that all those references were teaching relationship, not identity.

In Matthew 25, had the foolish virgins maintained a right relationship with the Bridegroom, they would not have been excluded from the marriage chamber. No one questions Jesus being the Bridegroom, but I must question that the virgins, wise or foolish, were to be the Bride. In the truest sense, they were friends of the Bridegroom. Some had maintained an up-to-date relationship with Him, while others had not.

Consider John 3:29 in which John the Baptist, speaking of Jesus, makes a profound statement: **He who has the bride is the bridegroom.** Apparently there were people who thought John the Baptist to be the Christ. Why would anyone think that?

Remember, John was the first direct voice from God to the Israelites after the ministry of Malachi more than 400 years before. During that period, the people had the writings of Moses and the prophets with which to direct themselves. However, the priesthood was virtually backslidden, and idolatry was an everyday form of religion. Few of the people remained true to God.

Among the faithful were the priest, Zacharias, and his wife, Elizabeth. (Luke 1:5-25.) Zacharias and Elizabeth were quite old when their son, John, was born. Among the youth who still loved and worshiped God were Mary and Joseph.

Now back to John's statement. Notice he said, **He** (Jesus) **who has (hath** KJV) **the bride is the bridegroom.** The word *has* (*hath* in KJV is the archaic form) is the present indicative of "have." "Have" in this verse indicates possession. The remainder of John's statement recognizes the friends of the Bridegroom as those who stand with Him, hear Him and rejoice. When researching New Testament

Church identity, one will find that those who stand, hear and rejoice are identified as the Church.

In Ephesians 5:24-30, carefully notice that these verses are describing the relationship between husband and wife, and do not lend themselves to one's identity. These Scriptures relate the Church to the Body of Christ, therefore making the Church a definite part of Jesus, the Bridegroom.

The identity of the Church as the Bride of Christ often prevents one from ever developing a strong, loving relationship with Jesus.

Throughout his epistles, the apostle Paul not only identifies the Church as the Body of Christ of which Christ is the Head, but he tells us that we wear armor. (See Eph. 6:10-17.) In Second Corinthians 10:4 he instructs us to use those weapons that are **mighty in God for pulling down strongholds.** Then he speaks, by the Holy Spirit, to Timothy and identifies him as **a good soldier of Jesus Christ** (2 Tim. 2:3).

We in the Body of Christ are involved in spiritual warfare. Armor and weapons are necessary and vital to every believer, along with the proper instructions as to how we are to wear and use that which God has supplied. Revelation 19:14 further identifies us as an army, the same company called saints in Zechariah 14:5. Notice how in both places we are returning to the earth from heaven. We go up to heaven as victorious soldiers and return to earth with the same identity.

What more need I write? It is very evident that we, the Church, are not the Bride, but rather God's army in the world.

Someone has suggested that although we are presently believing soldiers, who are wearing armor and using weapons, we might become the Bride once we are taken up to heaven. My conclusion is based on Revelation 19:14

God's Master Performance

which shows the Church returning as the army of our Lord Jesus, not as His Bride.

Allow me to strongly urge every believer to recognize our identity as the Body of Christ and then work toward developing a wonderful relationship with Jesus.

Since it is biblically evident that the Church is not the Bride, then who is? For this information, one has to go to the book of Revelation, chapters 19 and 21.

Revelation 19:7 reads: **Let *us* be glad and rejoice and give Him glory, for the marriage of the Lamb has come, and His wife has made herself ready.** The opening verses set the location for the scene and the multitude present. Verse 7 addresses that multitude, making it clear that the Bride and the multitude are not one and the same. Notice also that the Bride, or Lamb's wife, is adorned with **fine linen...the righteous acts of the saints** (v. 8).

Let's remain with the book of Revelation and proceed to chapter 21. Begin carefully to read verse 1 and continue through verse 11. John, by the Holy Spirit, simply declares the city, New Jerusalem, to be the Lamb's wife, or Bride, according to Revelation 21, verses 2, 9 and 10. As you continue the study of chapters 21 and 22, you realize the New Jerusalem is no ordinary city. It cannot be compared with any city built by men.

We are programmed to think of a city as something like New York, Chicago, Los Angeles, Houston or the city of our natural birth. However, the New Jerusalem is the city associated with our new birth. It is supernatural and unlike any natural, existing city.

One may reason, *How can a city be the Bride of Christ?* The simplest answer is: this is the revelation the Holy Spirit gave to John. By faith, we must accept the revelation. Remember, **we walk by faith, not by sight** (2 Cor. 5:7).

210

One may say, *I don't understand and I need understanding.* Again, I remind all of us that we are saved by grace through faith (Eph. 2:8), and no one can explain the new birth any better than the Scripture. We live by faith and, with the faith God has given us, believe the written Word.

If one isn't careful, it would be easy to take a "Thomas position" in relationship to the New Jerusalem as the Bride of Christ. Thomas' position was, "I can't believe until I have understanding through my natural senses." (See John 20:25.)

Do not confuse the *identity* of the Church, which is the Body of Christ, with the *relationship* we must develop. Both are made very clear in the Scriptures.

It is possible this teaching about the identity of the Bride crosses swords with your traditional position. If so, only you can decide whether you will stay with tradition or allow the Word of God to speak for itself.

For the present, let us put on the whole armor of God, take up the mighty weapons of God as good soldiers, and by faith carry out our assignment as the army and Body of Christ in this present world.

Whether you agree or disagree with the identity of the Bride of Christ will not affect your salvation, but it could affect your Christian lifestyle. I have met multitudes of Christians who seldom wear armor or use God's weapons. Rarely do they attack Satan or do his kingdom any harm. In fact, Satan beats, cheats and robs them on a regular basis. The reason for the above condition is the lack of true identity and a failure to develop a proper relationship with Jesus.

One last provoking question: *If the Church is the Bride of Christ, as is often taught, why was John shown something different?* I rest my case!

The New Jerusalem

> And he carried me away in the Spirit to a great and high mountain, and showed me the great city, the holy Jerusalem, descending out of heaven from God, having the glory of God. Her light was like a most precious stone, like a jasper stone, clear as crystal.
>
> Also she had a great and high wall with twelve gates, and twelve angels at the gates, and names written on them, which are the names of the twelve tribes of the children of Israel: three gates on the east, three gates on the north, three gates on the south, and three gates on the west.
>
> Now the wall of the city had twelve foundations, and on them were the names of the twelve apostles of the Lamb (vv. 10-14).

So the Lamb's Bride, His wife, is the New Jerusalem, occupied by God the Father, Jesus the Son and the Body of Christ, the Church.

Chronologically, the Wedding of the Lamb and the following Marriage Supper occur during the last four years of the Tribulation. The New Jerusalem comes to rest upon the new earth after the Great White Throne Judgment, which follows the Tribulation and the Millennium.

John describes the New Jerusalem as it comes down from God in heaven. The city is majestic — beautiful like a jasper stone! Clear as crystal! It has a great, high wall around it with an angel at each of its twelve gates.

Its Occupants

We know a large company of Old and New Testament glorified saints occupy this beautiful city.[1] Three gates are on the east of the city; three on the north, south and west. The names of the twelve tribes of Israel are written over the

---

[1] Because of Jesus' death, burial and resurrection, the Old Testament righteous became part of the dead in Christ. (See Luke 23:43; Eph. 4:8; Matt. 17:1-8.)

gates. The wall of the city has twelve foundations in which the names of the Lamb's twelve apostles are written. God's plan is magnificent.

Its Size

And he who talked with me had a gold reed to measure the city, its gates, and its wall. The city is laid out as a square; its length is as great as its breadth. And he measured the city with the reed: twelve thousand furlongs. Its length, breadth, and height are equal (vv. 15,16).

The New Jerusalem is 1,500 *miles square*, not *square miles*. This is the equivalent of 2,250,000 square miles per level.[2] Los Angeles, the largest American city in land area, covers more than 500 square miles. The New Jerusalem is 1,500 miles north to south, east to west, and 1,500 miles high! If it were placed on the United States, it would fit laterally between the Rocky and Appalachian Mountains, longitudinally between the Canadian border and the Gulf of Mexico. This is not a country or state, but a city — and it is still 1,500 miles high!

Some people preach that so few of us will be in this vast city we might not see another child of God for years. Jesus said His Father's house will be filled. (See Luke 14:16-24.) That enormous city, capable of holding multitudes of people, will be full. What a blessed fellowship this will be!

The Church has a great job to do in this hour! Its members must rid themselves of their fears, frustrations and negative attitudes, allowing the Holy Spirit to energize them to work for Jesus!

The city wall is extremely tall:

Then he measured its wall: one hundred and forty-four cubits, according to the measure of a man, that is, of an angel (v. 17).

[2]Nothing in Scripture gives insight as to how many levels there may be.

One hundred forty-four cubits is approximately 216 feet. The height of the city's wall is equivalent to that of a twenty-two-story building.

Its Elegance

> The construction of its wall was of jasper; and the city was pure gold, like clear glass. The foundations of the wall of the city were adorned with all kinds of precious stones: the first foundation was jasper, the second sapphire, the third chalcedony, the fourth emerald, the fifth sardonyx, the sixth sardius, the seventh chrysolite, the eighth beryl, the ninth topaz, the tenth chrysoprase, the eleventh jacinth, and the twelfth amethyst.
>
> The twelve gates were twelve pearls: each individual gate was of one pearl. And the street of the city was pure gold, like transparent glass. But I saw no temple in it... (vv. 18-22).

Twelve magnificent foundations, each formed from a solid precious stone, support the wall made of jasper. Each foundation is garnished with the stones of the other eleven. The city is made of pure gold.

Each gate, made of a single pearl, in a wall that runs 1,500 miles in one direction and stands about twenty-two stories high will be magnificent! The gates will have to be massive to fit architecturally. One theologian speculated that each gate will be 100 miles wide. We'll have to wait and see.

The streets are not *paved* with gold, as some songs declare, but *are* pure gold!

Its Temple

> But I saw no temple in it, for the Lord God Almighty and the Lamb are its temple (v. 22).

As we saw, Revelation 4:11 NKJV states that by God's will all things were created and exist; KJV translates this verse as God created all things for His pleasure. The overcoming believers who occupy the New Jerusalem are the ones who have brought Him the most pleasure, so He moves right in with them. God and Jesus dwell in the same city with us!

Because of the personal presence of God and Jesus, there is no need for a place of worship in the New Jerusalem. This should not be interpreted to mean that today's believers need no house of worship. God ordered the construction of the tabernacle in the wilderness and the temples of Israel in Jerusalem.[3] In these places the very glory of God was manifested.

Early believers met in their homes until either growth or persecution drove them into an open arena. God has used many homes to start fellowships. His plan is for the Body of Christ to grow. If a small group pleases God, it will grow, making a larger sanctuary soon necessary.

The church sanctuary can be a renovated car dealership, a supermarket, a discount store, a large metal building or a brick structure. Such a place becomes the vital center for worship and teaching around which believers flow in harmony, doing business for God throughout their community. When with others, one can easily enter into worship.

Knowing human nature better than man does, God has ordained that we Christians should meet in specific houses to worship. The apostle Paul declares that as we see the Day of the Lord approaching, we ought to assemble ourselves together all the more. (Heb. 10:25.)

Greater assemblies of God's children are appearing in every city. We are learning to love one another, work together, have fellowship and are finally beginning to

---

[3]Exodus 25:8; First Kings 6:1,2; Ezra 3.

experience and teach the same things. The Church is being ministered to by the elders whom God has set in it for the perfecting of the saints.

The strong local Church should operate together rather than splitting into small religious cliques. Often overcome by pride, these "bless me clubs" have no strength to do the devil much harm and sometimes become the source of erroneous teachings. In coming together, the Church finds protection, soundness and an abundance of good counsel. (Heb. 10:25; Prov. 11:14.)

Its Source of Light

> The city had no need of the sun or of the moon to shine in it, for the glory of God illuminated it. The Lamb is its light.
> And the nations of those who are saved shall walk in its light, and the kings of the earth bring their glory and honor into it (vv. 23,24).

The Source of energy for lighting the city is the glory of God and the Lamb, Jesus! They outshine the sun!

We know the New Jerusalem has come from heaven to rest upon the new earth. It is occupied by God the Father, God the Son and the Church company. The righteous people of the new earth walk in its light and go in and out through its gates. These righteous nations have kings who at appropriate times bring their glory and honor into the city, indicating that these are times of rejoicing and celebration. The people will joyfully anticipate those times as we do our major holidays.

Its Righteousness

> Its gates shall not be shut at all by day (there shall be no night there). And they shall bring the glory and the honor of the nations into it. But there shall by no means enter it anything that defiles, or causes an abomination or a lie, but only those who are written in the Lamb's Book of Life (vv. 25-27).

Verse 27 of this chapter reveals that those people who defile, work abominations or lie have already been cast into the lake of fire. They have no part with the new heaven, new earth or New Jerusalem.

Combined together on the new earth are:

...a righteous people in mortal bodies like Adam and Eve before the Fall.

...the nation of Israel, fully restored during the Millennium, occupied by the natural seed of Abraham in mortal bodies. (See Isa. 35; Ezek. 36:11.)

...the Church, the only inhabitants with glorified bodies who live in New Jerusalem and continue serving as administrators of Jesus' everlasting kingdom.

One must keep in mind that everything God has done was and is perfect. Although Satan hindered God's plan in the Garden of Eden, the plan was no less perfect. The Father chose Abraham and his seed through which to bless all nations. The plan was perfect even though Satan tampered with it.

God preserves every phase of His perfect plan. He does so in the Millennium by having righteous people in mortal bodies occupying the new earth. He has the seed of Abraham creating a perfect nation called Israel. He has a third company made of believers with glorified bodies establishing that we through Jesus Christ overcome Satan. (We believers should not allow Satan to overcome us as did Adam and Eve and the natural seed of Abraham.)

God has not changed His mind about having a perfect mortal being. Neither has He changed His mind about having a perfect nation of people such as Israel. God is bringing His Church into perfection through the ministry of apostles, prophets, evangelists, pastors and teachers.

(Eph. 4:11-16.) Therefore, we overcome and, as part of the reward, are given glorified bodies so that we are just like Jesus! (1 Cor. 15:51-53; 1 John 3:1-3.)

God has brought every part of His plan together on the new earth. What a beautiful scene!

20

Revelation 22
Informational

And he showed me a pure river of water of life, clear as crystal, proceeding from the throne of God and of the Lamb. In the middle of its street, and on either side of the river, was the tree of life, which bore twelve fruits, each tree yielding its fruit every month. The leaves of the tree were for the healing of the nations (vv. 1,2).

This description of the clear water of the River of Life flowing from God's throne shows there is absolutely no pollution in the New Jerusalem, or on the new earth.

The golden street in the New Jerusalem is actually a boulevard. The River of Life flows down the middle of it, and the Trees of Life, the only species of tree in the entire city, grow on both banks. This tree bears twelve kinds of fruit and produces every month. Its fruit is to be eaten by the overcoming believers. (Rev. 2:7.)

Paul gives us insight into the magnificence of the New Jerusalem. He writes: **But as it is written: "Eye has not seen, nor ear heard, nor have entered into the heart of man the things which God has prepared for those who love Him"** (1 Cor. 2:9).

The Food of Heaven

Often people ask, "Since our bodies will be glorified, will we eat in heaven?"

Yes, we will eat at the Marriage Supper of the Lamb, during the Millennium and in the New Jerusalem. Following His resurrection, Jesus in His glorified body ate fish and bread with His disciples. He even cooked for them.

In heaven we will not eat because we need nourishment or because we are hungry. We will have the pleasure of eating God's special fruit of the Tree of Life.

The Eighth Unknown

...The leaves of the tree were for the healing of the nations (v. 2). Our understanding of this verse is limited. We know that everyone who eats of the Tree of Life will have unending health. (See Gen. 3:22-24.) The nations of this verse are the ones which occupy the new earth and have access to the city. Since there is no sickness or disease, the leaves maintain life as they would have for Adam.

The Church company, serving as kings and priests, possessing total knowledge, will certainly have full understanding as to the healing effect of the leaves of the Tree of Life.

Keep the Sayings of Revelation

And there shall be no more curse, but the throne of God and of the Lamb shall be in it, and His servants shall serve Him. They shall see His face, and His name shall be on their foreheads.

There shall be no night there: They need no lamp nor light of the sun, for the Lord God gives them light. And they shall reign forever and ever.

Then he said to me, "These words are faithful and true." And the Lord God of the holy prophets sent His angel to show His servants the things which must shortly take place.

"Behold, I am coming quickly! Blessed is he who keeps the words of the prophecy of this book" (vv. 3-7).

With verse 7 the prophecy that began in Revelation 4 closes. Verses 8 through 21 conclude John's cover letter of Revelation 1. This letter conveys the final remarks which the Lord directed John to speak to the seven churches in Asia. These statements are also directed to the Church as a whole until the end of the Church Age.

> **Now I, John, saw and heard these things. And when I heard and saw, I fell down to worship before the feet of the angel who showed me these things. Then he said to me, "See that you do not do that. For I am your fellow servant, and of your brethren the prophets, and of those who keep the words of this book. Worship God" (vv. 8,9).**

The theme of this book is Jesus. The book reveals the last act of God's master performance. It emphasizes that we are to worship the only true God Who created heaven and earth; the God of Abraham, Isaac, Jacob, Peter, James, John and Paul; the God Who gave us the only Savior, Jesus Christ; the God Who provides for those who accept His Son. Worship God — not man! Worship the Creator — not the creature, nor money and things!

Revelation Is Not Sealed

> **And he said to me, "Do not seal the words of the prophecy of this book, for the time is at hand" (v. 10).**

Daniel's prophecies were sealed until **the time of the end.** That seal has been lifted! The Revelation was never sealed. John writes, ...**the time *is* at hand.** This statement also appears in Revelation 1:3. John sent the prophecy to the seven churches with the intention that its distribution be continued. He admonished the churches to keep the things written in the prophecy. This instruction applies to every succeeding generation of the Church.

Until recently, Revelation was approached with intellectualism, carnal understanding or fear. God's Word cannot be interpreted by those means but only by the Holy Spirit. Today we are living in the time of the end, as taught by Daniel in chapter 12. The Holy Spirit is causing a Word explosion. He is changing our theology, doctrine and attitude. We are growing in God's Word, and our understanding is becoming increasingly more fruitful.

He who is unjust, let him be unjust still; he who is filthy, let him be filthy still; he who is righteous, let him be righteous still; he who is holy, let him be holy still (v. 11).

The prophecy of this book will not change all unrighteous people into righteous ones or afford the righteous any greater tools than are already available. The prophecy will eventually affect all people. But whether or not they change their course, the prophecy must be declared.

And behold, I am coming quickly, and My reward is with Me, to give to every one according to his work (v. 12).

There are two kinds of judgment — good and bad, in favor or against. The judgment seat of Christ is favorable. When one is raptured, he has already been judged righteous and victorious, ready for the event. No one will be raptured unless God's favor is already upon him.

When Jesus comes to catch up His own, He brings their rewards with Him. This is a judgment of rewards, so go to work! No one is saved by works, but works determine the reward of the righteous.

"I am the Alpha and the Omega, the Beginning and the End, the First and the Last."

Blessed are those who do His commandments, that they may have the right to the tree of life, and may enter through the gates into the city.

For outside are dogs and sorcerers and sexually immoral and murderers and idolaters, and whoever loves and practices a lie (vv. 13-15).

Here is another passage which indicates the unrighteous will not inhabit the new earth. The statements in this verse and Revelation 21:8,27 are warnings to those who habitually participate in the activities described.

Do Not Alter the Word

"I, Jesus, have sent My angel to testify to you these things in the churches. I am the Root and the Offspring of David, the Bright and Morning Star."

And the Spirit and the bride say, "Come!" And let him who hears say, "Come!" And let him who thirsts come. Whoever desires, let him take the water of life freely.

For I testify to everyone who hears the words of the prophecy of this book: If anyone adds to these things, God will add to him the plagues that are written in this book; and if anyone takes away from the words of the book of this prophecy, God shall take away his part from the Book of Life, from the holy city, and from the things which are written in this book (vv. 16-19).

This passage contains a strong admonition not to tamper with any part of God's Word. Since Revelation is tied into both the Old and New Testaments, this warning covers the entire Bible.

Declaring that part of the Word has been done away with or that certain portions are not for us today is tampering with the Word. Such action is flirting with disaster.

God's Love Is With Us

He who testifies to these things says, "Surely I am coming quickly." Amen. Even so, come, Lord Jesus! The grace of our Lord Jesus Christ be with you all. Amen (vv. 20,21).

The Revelation closes on a magnificent note: It assures us of Jesus' glorious return and reminds us that His love is constantly with us while we await the event. Let us grow in the grace and knowledge of the Lord unto full maturity, in which there are no divisions, and enjoy unity of faith and complete knowledge of the Son of God.

Conclusion

We have joyfully discovered that Revelation is a continuation of the New Testament description of Jesus and His ministry, not a volume of doom and gloom. The Antichrist, False Prophet and mark of the Beast are no threat to the glorious Church and are of minor importance in the story of God's master performance.

The book of Revelation has proven itself to be the exciting last chapter, final act and grand finale of the most successful Book in existence — the Holy Bible.

Appendixes

Appendix 1
The Unknowns of Revelation

The unknowns are not explained anywhere within scriptural context. Therefore, understanding is withheld until our knowledge is complete. When we see Jesus, we will be like Him, as stated in First John 3:2. Then we shall have total knowledge.

1. The significance of the four creatures' strange appearance. (Rev. 4.)

2. The personal identity of the white horse's rider. (Rev. 6.)

3. The reason for the half hour of silence. (Rev. 8.)

4. The nature and purpose of the seven thunders. (Rev. 10:3,4.)

5. John's future ministry. (Rev. 10:11.)

6. The personal identity of the Two Witnesses. (Rev. 11.)

7. The area covered by the wilderness where the Israeli remnant is hidden and the origin of the eagle's wings. (Rev. 12:14.)

8. The exact effect of the leaves of the Tree of Life. (Rev. 22:2.)

Appendix 2
An Overview of Revelation

Rev. 1,2,3	Introduction and message to the seven churches.
Rev. 4,5	Catching up of the Church. Scene before God's throne. Identification of the 24 elders. Jesus' receiving the book with 7 seals.
Rev. 6	Opening of the first 6 seals. The first: White horse — Antichrist. The second: Red horse — war, World War III. (Ezek. 38,39.) The third: Black horse — famine. The fourth: Pale Horse — Death (accompanied by Hell). The fifth: Martyred Tribulation saints. The sixth: Upheaval of nature reserved until end of Tribulation.

Rev. 7	Two groups revealed.
	  The 144,000 Jewish evangelists who begin ministry early in
	    Tribulation's first year. (vv. 1-8.) (Rev. 14:1-5; Ezek. 9:4.)
	  The Great Multitude (mid-Tribulation saints) caught up to
	    God's throne. (v. 9.)

	Mid-Tribulation. (See Appendix 3.)

Rev. 8,9,10	Seventh seal: Ushers in 7 trumpet judgments.
	First-Fourth: Plagues used intermittently throughout 3 1/2 years.
	Fifth: First woe — Demon locusts, no death, five-month duration.
	  (Rev. 9.)
	Sixth: Second woe — Eastern army destroyed at Armageddon.
	  (Rev. 9.)
	Seventh: Third woe — Reserved until end of Tribulation. (Rev. 11.)

	Two Witnesses. (Rev. 11.) Israel escapes to wilderness. (Rev. 12.) Mark of the Beast. (Rev. 13.) Angelic ministry. (Rev. 8:13; 14:6-20.)
Rev. 14	The 144,000 finish ministry and appear with Christ. No further reference in story.
Rev. 15,16	Last 7 plagues, approximately 30 days. Insight to Armageddon. (Rev. 14:14-20; 16:16; 19:11-21; Zech. 14.)
Rev. 19	Christ returns with His saints. (Zech. 14:5; Rev. 17:14.) Battle of Armageddon. (Rev. 19:11-21; Zech. 14.) Antichrist and False Prophet cast into lake of fire. (Rev. 19:20.)
Rev. 20	1,000-year reign of Jesus Christ on earth. Martyrs are resurrected. Saints reign as kings and priests. Satan is bound for 1,000 years. Israel is totally restored. (Isa. 35; Ezek. 36.)
Rev. 20:7-10	Release of Satan. Final battle with Satan.
Rev. 20:11-15	Final resurrection of wicked dead. White Throne Judgment.
Rev. 21,22	New Jerusalem, new heaven and new earth.

Horsemen ride throughout Tribulation.

3 1/2 years

Seven years of Tribulation (also called Daniel's 70th Week or Jacob's trouble).*

---

*Jacob's trouble (Jer. 30:7) refers to the last half of the seven-year period.

Appendix 3
Mid-Tribulation Events

1. Antichrist breaks agreement with Israel. (Dan. 9:24-27.)

2. Tribulation saints (Jews and Gentiles) caught up and escape wrath of Antichrist. (Rev. 7:9-17.)

3. Upheaval of nature. (Rev. 8:5.)

4. Antichrist moves against Israel; remnant of Israel hidden away. (Dan. 9; Rev. 12:13-17.)

5. Antichrist destroys the religious system (world church harlot). (Rev. 17:16-18.)

6. Antichrist declares himself God. (2 Thess. 2:3,4.)

7. False Prophet introduces mark of the Beast and attempts to control commerce. (Rev. 13:16-18.)

8. False Prophet introduces idolatry — worship of the image. (Rev. 13:14,15.)

9. Two Witnesses begin ministry. (Rev. 11.)

10. Angelic ministry begins. (Rev. 14:6-9.)

11. Plagues begin. (Rev. 8,9.)

Appendix 4
Nature's Upheaval
During the Tribulation

1. At Tribulation's beginning.
   (Occurs during World War III which follows the
   Rapture of the Church.)
   > Earthquake. (Ezek. 38:19,20.)
   > Thunder, lightning. (Rev. 4:5.)

2. At mid-Tribulation. (Rev. 8:5.)

3. On Tribulation's final day.
   Opening of sixth seal (reserved until this time).
   (Rev. 6:12-17.)
   At resurrection of Two Witnesses. (Rev. 11:13.)
   At time of Armageddon. (Zech. 14:4,6-8.)
   Pouring out of seventh vial. (Rev. 16:17-20.)

Appendix 5
Summary
Last Day of the Great Tribulation
and
1,000-Year Reign of Christ

On the last day of the Tribulation, a tremendous upheaval of nature occurs. (Rev. 6:12-17; 11:13-19; 16:18-21.) A great earthquake alters the shape of the earth, perhaps returning the earth to its rightful position on its axis. The Two Witnesses, slain three-and-one-half days previously and left lying in the streets of Jerusalem, are miraculously brought back to life. Men actually hear God's voice as He calls the witnesses back to His throne. (Rev. 11:7-12.)

The world is thrown into tremendous fear because on this day ...**there will be no light; the lights will diminish. It shall be one day which is known to the Lord — neither day nor night. But at evening time it shall happen that it will be light** (Zech. 14:6,7).

Jesus returns as the King of kings and Lord of lords with millions of His saints to battle against the Antichrist and his armies in the Battle of Armageddon. (Rev. 19:16,19.) The armies of the evil one are destroyed in a horrible manner. (Zech. 14:9,12.) Satan is bound by an angel and cast into the bottomless pit for 1,000 years. (Rev. 20:1-3.)

The Tribulation's last day marks the first day of the Millennium, Jesus' 1,000-year reign of peace. During the

Millennium, Jesus and His saints rule over the nations which were not controlled by the Antichrist. Zechariah 14:16 reveals that within the nations controlled by the Antichrist there are people who have not taken his mark nor worshiped the image of the Beast.

During the 1,000-year reign of Christ, people will continue reproducing. On this last day of the Tribulation and first day of the Millennium, the saved remnant of Israel (Rev. 11:13) is gathered from its hiding place and the Tribulation martyrs are resurrected. (Rev. 20:4.)

The 1,000-year reign of Christ is one of total peace and righteousness, in which much restoration of the earth takes place. The nation of Israel is restored to its original estate. (Ezek. 36:11.)

Appendix 6
Chronological Development
of the Beast System
(Rev. 12,13,17,18; Dan. 2,7)

The Original Heads

1. Babylon (Egypt)
2. Assyria
3. Babylon
   Daniel's prophecy begins. (Dan. 2.)
4. Medo-Persia
5. Greece
6. Rome
   Mortally wounded and later revived as the seventh head of the system. (Rev. 13.)*

The first coming of Jesus brings the Church Age — the stone destroys the image. (Dan. 2:35.)

The Church is caught up.

The Final Heads

7. Common Market of Europe
   10 horns
8. Antichrist
   Final 3 1/2 years of the Tribulation, 10 horns

---

*The Beast's heads are empires. The Roman Empire, a combination of the other heads, became the whole system. It requires the shrewd Antichrist to assemble the governments, commerce and religions of the Beast to resurrect it. *Note*: The total system, not just the Roman Empire, is revived.

Appendix 7

The Seven-Year Tribulation Period

A. Daniel's 70th Week (Dan. 9:24-27)

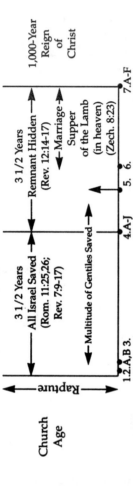

Church Age

Rapture

3 1/2 Years — All Israel Saved (Rom. 11:25,26; Rev. 7:9-17)

Multitude of Gentiles Saved

3 1/2 Years — Remnant Hidden (Rev. 12:14-17)

Marriage Supper of the Lamb (in heaven) (Zech. 8:23)

1,000-Year Reign of Christ

1,2.A,B 3.   4.A-J   5. 6.   7.A-F

1. Rapture of the Church. (Luke 21:36; John 14:3; 1 Thess. 4:16-18; 2 Thess. 2:1-9; Rev. 4:1-3.)
2. Opening of the Seals. (Rev. 6.)
   A. Release of the Antichrist. (Dan. 9:24-27; Rev. 6:1,2.)
   B. Destruction of Russia, World War III. (Ezek. 38,39; Rev. 6:3,4.)
3. Selection of the 144,000 and the beginning of their ministry. (Ezek. 9:1-6; Rev. 7:1-8; 14:1-5.)
4. Mid-Tribulation.
   A. Agreement broken with Israel. (Dan. 9:24-27.)
   B. Rapture of the Great Multitude. (Rev. 7:9-17.)
   C. Upheaval of nature. (Rev. 8:5.)
   D. Antichrist moves against Israel. (Dan. 9.)
   E. Antichrist destroys the harlot. (Rev. 17:16-18.)
   F. Antichrist press conference. (2 Thess. 2:3,4.)
   G. Mark of the Beast introduced. (Rev. 13:16-18.)
   H. Two Witnesses. (Rev. 11:3-12.)
   I. Ministry of angels. (Rev. 14:6-12.)
   J. Plagues. (Rev. 8,9.)
5. Rapture of the 144,000. (Rev. 14:1-5.)
6. Marriage of the Lamb (in heaven). (Rev. 19:1-9.)
7. Final Day.
   A. Rapture of the Two Witnesses. (Rev. 11:3-12.)
   B. Christ returns. (Zech. 14; Rev. 19.)
   C. Armageddon. (Rev. 19:19-21.)
   D. Antichrist and False Prophet cast into the lake of fire. (Rev. 19:20.)
   E. Satan bound. (Rev. 20:1-3.)
   F. Christ reigns. (Rev. 20:4; Isa. 9:6.)

Appendix 7
The Seven-Year Tribulation Period
B. Terms *Last Days* and
Time of the End
Cover the Tribulation

The seven years designated by Daniel in chapter 9, verses 24-27, correspond to the same period of time covered in the book of Revelation and identified by Jesus in Matthew 24 as "the Tribulation."

These seven years are an exact period of time — 84 months or 2,520 days — divided into two equal halves of three-and-one-half years, 42 months or 1,260 days. Each month of that time is exactly 30 days long.

"And It Shall Come to Pass"

Besides the phrases *last days* and *time of the end*, there is another prophetic term I want to consider: *And it shall come to pass....* We find these words 131 times in both Old and New Testaments.

God spoke through Joel:

> *And it shall come to pass* **afterward that I will pour out My Spirit on all flesh.**
>
> Joel 2:28

Whenever God says, **And it shall come to pass...**, the words which follow that term are more sure and certain to occur than the rising and setting of the sun.

No one ever questions the rising and setting of the sun.

No one has ever asked, *Now that the sun is up, will it go down?*

Such thoughts never go through our minds.

From the time God created the sun and set it into action, it has risen and set every day (with the one exception given in Josh. 10:13).

We never think about such things because they are absolutes.

The same is true regarding God's prophetic Word. If God said it, it will come to pass. These days we are witnessing the action of God's Word as it comes to pass.

An elementary knowledge of Bible prophecy enables us to begin to realize how important are the fulfillments of the prophecies of the Scriptures. There can be no doubt that God is having His way. The Bible is literally coming to pass.

Appendix 8
Three Phases of Activity

Seals (Rev. 6)

1. White horse rider — Antichrist.
2. Red horse — war.
3. Black horse — famine (terrible, but not worldwide).
4. Pale horse — Death and Hell.
5. Martyred Tribulation saints.
6. The most severe upheaval of nature (on the Tribulation's final day).
7. Prepares the way for the sounding of the seven trumpets. (Rev. 8:1.)

Trumpets (Rev. 8,9,11)

1. Hail, fire, blood (rain).
2. Oceans become one-third blood.
3. Domestic water becomes one-third poisoned.
4. Darkness of one-third of the sun's, moon's and stars' light.
5. Plague of demon-driven locusts.
6. Movement of vast Oriental army.
7. Last angelic trumpet — Battle of Armageddon, return of Jesus Christ.

Vials (Rev. 16)

1. Boils.
2. Oceans become totally blood.
3. Domestic water becomes totally blood.
4. Heat of sun increased.
5. Total darkness of sun, moon and stars over Antichrist's kingdom.
6. The way of the Oriental army is prepared for its destruction at Armageddon.
7. Upheaval of nature (fulfillment of events resulting from opening of sixth seal).

239

Appendix 9
Chapter Subjects of Revelation

1. Introduction, John's cover letter to the seven churches of Asia.
2. Letters to the churches of Ephesus, Smyrna, Pergamos, Thyatira.
3. Letters to the churches of Sardis, Philadelphia, Laodicea.
*4. John caught up.
*5. The book with seven seals.
†6. Opening of the seals.
‡7. 144,000 and their converts.
†8. Sounding of trumpets.
†9. Plague of locusts, Oriental army.
‡10. Seven thunders, John's future.
‡11. Two Witnesses, seventh angelic trumpet.
‡12. Sun-clothed woman, male child, hidden remnant.
‡13. Seven-headed Beast — the System, Antichrist, False Prophet.
‡14. 144,000 caught up, angelic ministry, preview of Armageddon.
‡15. Introduction to Revelation 16.
†16. Last seven plagues.
‡17. The harlot.
*†‡18. The harlot's obituary.
*†‡19. Christ returns, Armageddon.
*†20. Satan bound, 1,000-year reign, White Throne Judgment.
‡21. New heaven, new earth, New Jerusalem.
‡22. New Jerusalem, conclusion of John's cover letter.

---

*Story of heaven †Story of earth ‡Informational chapters

Note: The story of chapter 19 begins in heaven and, with verse 11, moves to earth. The story of chapter 20 begins on earth and, with verse 11, moves to heaven.

Appendix 10
The First Resurrection
(Rev. 20:5,6)

1. Resurrection of dead in Christ at the appearing of Jesus. (1 Cor. 15:51,52; 1 Thess. 4:16.)

2. Catching up of living saints to meet Christ in the air. (1 Cor. 15:51,52; 1 Thess. 4:17.)

3. Catching up of the Great Multitude (mid-Tribulation saints). (Rev. 7:9.)

4. Catching up of 144,000 servants of God. (Rev. 14:1-5.)

5. Resurrection of the Two Witnesses. (Rev. 11.)

6. Catching up of the Two Witnesses. (Rev. 11.)

7. Resurrection of Tribulation martyrs. (Rev. 20:4,6.)

The Last Resurrection
and
White Throne Judgment

The wicked of all the ages. (Rev. 20:5,11-15.)

Appendix 11
Biblical Rules of Interpretation

The study of the Scriptures reveals several built-in rules that assist us with both proper interpretation and rightly dividing the Word of Truth. The first one to consider is the rule of double reference.

It becomes evident from the study of the Old Testament that there are many truths and instructions that also apply to the Church. Let us not forget that, although Jesus delivered us from the curse of the Law, He did not do away with the righteousness of the Law. Therefore, when one of the Old Testament writers sets forth righteous instructions, it is as much for us as it was for the people of Israel. Also, when God pronounced blessings, they are equally ours through Jesus Christ. (Gal. 3:13,14.) Since God is not a respecter of persons, He would not work miracles for Israel and not do the same for us.

We are also instructed to recognize the examples within the Old Testament of both the success and failures of Israel, thereby learning and benefiting from their record. (1 Cor. 10:11.)

Another rule of interpretation covers the use of the word *sea*. There are numerous times in which it refers to an existing body of water. When that is not the case, it will be identifying a mass of humanity — a sea of people.

When reading the Scripture and the word *sea* appears, examine the entire passage of Scripture sufficiently to determine whether it is indeed identifying a body of water or referring to masses of people.

The book of Revelation provides us some good examples. One is found in chapter 17 in which the harlot is described as "sitting upon many waters." The fifteenth verse of that chapter clearly describes the many waters as peoples, multitudes and nations.

First Samuel 13:5 provides us another excellent example of this rule, and there are a number more.

A similar rule covers the use of the word *mountain*. When reading Scripture in which the word *mountain* is used, if an existing mountain of rock is not identified by name or geographical location, then it is identifying a kingdom. The words *mountain* and *kingdom* become interchangeable.

An excellent example is found in Daniel, chapter 2, verses 34,35,44. You will notice that in verse 35 the word *mountain* is used, while in verse 44 the word *kingdom* is used, both identifying the same majestic act of the Almighty.

These simple rules will often enable you to have good understanding of the scriptural account.

About the Author:
John the Revelator

John the Revelator is none other than the apostle John, the Beloved Apostle. Who better to write this book than John?

John was one of the inner-circle disciples with Peter and James. One discovers, however, that John was probably closer to our Lord Jesus than the other two. It was not that Jesus loved him more but that John chose to be closer to Him.

John has given us the beloved gospel of John, which seems to stand out because of its loving revelation of Jesus. John captures God's love and divine provisions for the believer as does no other gospel writer. Through all of John's writing, Jesus is divinely described for you and me.

The Holy Spirit later used John to give us three marvelously wonderful epistles: First, Second and Third John. These epistles are filled with truths which are vital to everyday Christian living. John teaches us to love one another so we may fulfill the prayer of our Lord Jesus found in the gospel of John, chapter 17.

In John's very old age (93 to 96), he was still being used by God in a very dramatic way. We cannot be absolute on John's age, but it is generally accepted that he was in his mid-nineties when God permitted him to pen the book of Revelation. Senior citizens can be of great value to God and to the Church. By the time one becomes a senior, he should have learned much about God, His plan, His methods and His great love.

John was well-suited to author the book of Revelation. He could handle this insight into the future, which does reveal the outpouring of God's wrath. Because of the manner in which John was developed by the Holy Spirit, he was able to always cause God's love to be seen, even during the time when God releases His fierce wrath.

Although Jesus is the subject of the book of Revelation, the love of God is strong throughout the entire prophetic message.

Bibliography

1. *The Holy Bible.* Author: God, the I AM.

2. *The Book of Ezekiel.* Author: God through the prophet Ezekiel.

3. *The Book of Daniel.* Author: God through the prophet Daniel.

4. *The Book of Zechariah.* Author: God through the prophet Zechariah.

5. *The First and Second Epistles to the Corinthians.* Author: God through the apostle Paul.

6. *The Gospel of Luke.* Author: God through the apostle Luke, the physician.

7. *The First and Second Epistles to the Thessalonians.* Author: God through the apostle Paul.

8. *The Book of Revelation.* Author: God through the apostle John.

Index

Abraham, *34, 89, 93, 95, 217, 221*

Aegean Sea, *19, 33*

Angel, *18, 36-37, 42, 50, 52, 55-56, 60, 62, 73, 76, 89-90, 92, 100-101, 103, 105-107, 113-116, 122, 124, 132, 157, 167-171, 178-182, 192, 195, 212-213, 220-221, 223*

Angelic: company, *75-76*; host, *76*; ministry, *49, 124, 168*; trumpet, *116, 122, 125-126, 183*; trumpets, *126*; warfare, *136*

Angel's: declaration, *182*; instructions, *115*; trumpet call, *122*

Angels, *13, 24, 34-37, 39, 48, 56, 72, 75-77, 89-90, 93, 98-101, 106, 109, 123, 127, 133-136, 140, 155, 167-169, 172-173, 178, 201, 206, 212*; four, *89-90, 99-100, 106*; of the seven churches, *35-36*

Antichrist, *17, 19, 21, 80-83, 85, 87, 89, 93, 95, 97-99, 101, 108-109, 120-124, 133, 139-140, 144, 147-153, 160-164, 168-169, 171-172, 178-180, 183-184, 187, 191-193, 195, 197-199*; forces of, *140*;

Antichrist's: authority *180*; armies, *99, 124*; forces, *124*; right hand, *164*; wrath, *198*

Antichrist system, *21, 150*. *See also* Beast System *and* System (Antichrist or Beast)

Antipas, *50-51*

Apocalypse, (four) horsemen of, *80, 199*

Appearing, *32-33, 53, 58, 68-69, 80, 85, 95, 119, 126, 181, 215*

Appears, *32, 69, 71, 81, 87, 126, 139, 221*

Arab, *83*

Arabs, *150, 153*

Armageddon, *21, 85, 87, 98, 108-109, 122-124, 162, 170-172, 177, 181-184, 192-193*

Asia, *13, 31, 35, 39, 41, 108, 205, 221*

Asian areas, *181*

Assyria, *157*

Assyrian Empire, *157, 159*

Astrologers, *102, 132*

Astrology, *102, 110*

Babylon, *156, 164, 168, 182, 184*

Babylonian Empire, *145, 157, 159*

Battle, *21, 83, 87, 92, 98, 104-105, 109, 120, 122-124, 162, 170-172, 177, 181-182, 184, 193, 198-199*; of Armageddon,

Mountain, *86, 100, 158, 212*

Mountains, seven, *158, 161, 164*

Multitude, *89, 93-95, 124, 126, 139, 172, 188-189, 198, 210;* Great, *89, 93-95, 124, 126, 139, 172, 188-189, 198*

Nation, *23, 74, 93, 109, 139, 143, 149, 157, 167, 199, 217;* ten-nation confederacy, *162*

Nations, *48, 75, 81, 83-84, 91, 93-94, 97-99, 108-109, 116-117, 121, 123-124, 130-131, 133, 148-149, 153, 155, 161-163, 165, 167-168, 173, 180, 182, 192, 195, 197-199, 201, 216-217, 219-220*

Nebuchadnezzar, *145, 147, 157-159*

Nebuchadnezzar's dream, *145, 147, 157-158*

New: earth, *25, 197, 201-203, 205, 212, 216-220, 223;* heaven, *201-203, 205, 217;* heavens, *25;* Jerusalem, *25, 48, 60, 201, 203, 205, 210-213, 215-217, 219-220;* song, *74-75, 91-92, 95, 190*

Northern power, *92, 199*

Nuclear, *188*

Olive: branch, *93;* tree, *69, 93;* trees, *119*

Olives, Mount of, *87, 171, 192-193*

144,000, *89-95, 97-98, 103-105, 119, 123-124, 133, 139, 149-150, 167-168, 185, 189-190, 198;* 144,000 Jewish evangelists, *89, 95, 97, 133, 139, 149-150, 167-168, 189, 210*

1000-year: period, *199;* reign, *26, 33, 87, 125, 127, 173, 193*

One thousand years, *125, 196*

Orient, *107, 171*

Oriental army, *109, 124, 181, 199. See also* 200 million, army of

Orientals, *109, 124*

Overcomer, *47, 49-52, 56, 60-61, 205*

Overcomers, *47-50, 130, 205*

Pakistani-Indian war, *108*

Pakistanis, *109*

Paradise, *36, 47-48, 69*

Patmos, Isle of, *19, 33, 116*

Pergamos, *35, 41, 50-51*

Philadelphian church, church of Philadelphia, *56, 59*

Plague: *101-104, 120, 124, 171, 178-180, 183, 190, 192;* of locusts, *103, 190*

Throne (Continued)
48, 50, 61, 65, 67-76, 79, 82, 85-86, 91-94, 99-100, 104, 120, 130-131, 134-135, 144, 149, 167, 172-173, 180, 182, 188-189, 196-197, 200-201, 206, 212, 219-220; Great, *172;* Great White, *197, 200-201, 212*

Thrones, *69, 75, 95, 124, 196*

Thunders, seven, *113-114*

Thyatira, church of Thyatira, *35, 41, 52-53*

Time of the end, *24, 145-146, 221-222*

Times of the Gentiles, *145*

Tree of Life, *47-48, 219-220, 222*

Trees of Life, *219*

Tribes: northern, *157;* southern, *157;* twelve, *91, 212*

Tribulation, *24, 27, 33, 50, 52, 58-59, 66, 75, 80-85, 87, 89-90, 92-95, 97-102, 104, 108-110, 114, 116-117, 119-127, 130, 133, 138-139, 141, 148-149, 152-153, 161-162, 167, 171-172, 177-180, 182-185, 190, 197-199, 201, 212;* final day of the, *98, 109, 122-123, 126, 162, 178, 183-184, 198;* first half of the, *95, 97, 133;* great, *52, 94;* martyred saints of the, *179, 197;* martyrs, *84,*

Tribulation (Continued)
125; saints, *98, 184, 198, 201;* second half of the, *85, 116, 123;* last half of the, *100-101, 116, 127, 138-139, 148, 167;* seventh year of the, *109.* See also Mid-Tribulation

Tribulation Period, *24, 27, 58-59, 80-82, 87, 97, 100, 114, 116, 124, 126*

Tribulation's: end, *114, 123, 199;* final day, *116, 162;* last day, *116, 127;* final month, *109, 171-172, 177, 185;* last month, *108-109, 180*

Trumpet, *34-36, 65-66, 101-103, 106-107, 114, 116, 122, 124-126, 140, 167, 179-183;* of God, *66, 125-126*

Trumpets, *99-100, 102, 122, 125-126*

Twelve, *69, 91, 108, 117, 129, 161, 212-214, 219;* disciples, *117;* tribes, *91, 212*

12,000, *91*

Twenty-four, *68-71, 74-76, 124, 188*

200 million, (army of), *106, 108*

Two Witnesses, *85, 98-99, 101, 116-117, 119-120, 122-125, 127, 168, 184-185, 198*

United States, *15, 139, 196, 213*

Hilton Sutton is regarded by many people as the nation's foremost authority on Bible prophecy as related to current events and world affairs.

As an ordained minister of the Gospel, Dr. Sutton served as pastor for several years before entering his present prophetic assignment. Today he travels throughout the world, teaching and preaching God's Word. He takes the words of the most accurate news report ever — the Word of God — and relates it to the news today.

Having spent over thirty years researching and studying the book of Revelation, Hilton explains Bible prophecy and world affairs to the people in a way that is clear, concise and easy to understand. He presents his messages on a layman's level and shows the Bible to be the most accurate, up-to-date Book ever written.

Hilton and his family make their home in Humble, Texas, where he serves as president of Mission to America, a Christian organization dedicated to carrying the Gospel of Jesus Christ to the world. He is also president of Hilton Sutton Ministries and of an interdenominational ministerial and church fellowship, World Ministry Fellowship of Dallas, Texas. In addition, he is the national president of the Christian Evangelical Zionist Congress of America and serves on the board of the National Christian Leadership Conference for Israel of New York City.

Hilton covers several aspects of ministry outreach. His weekly telecast, "Vital Signs," can be seen on various Christian television stations. Besides authoring numerous books, he has created scores of audio tapes on the subject of prophecies of the Scripture.

To receive Hilton Sutton's
monthly publication, *Update*,
write:

Mission to America
Hilton Sutton Ministries
736 Wilson Road
Humble, Texas 77338

*Please include your prayer requests
and comments when you write.*

Other Books by Hilton Sutton

ABCs of Bible Prophecy

Death of an Empire —
The Prophetic Destiny
of the Soviet Union

Familiar Spirits, Witchcraft and Satanism
Innocent Beginnings, Deadly Results

Pre-Tribulation Rapture of the Church

Rapture, Get Right or Get Left

U.S. in Prophetic Events

Available from your local bookstore.

Harrison House
Tulsa, OK 74153

In Canada, contact:

Word Alive
P. O. Box 670
Niverville, Manitoba
CANADA R0A 1E0

The Harrison House Vision

Proclaiming the truth and the power
Of the Gospel of Jesus Christ
With excellence;

Challenging Christians to
Live victoriously,
Grow spiritually,
Know God intimately.